God Our Refuge

Devotions, Meditations, Gospel-Readings, Prayers, Hymns, and Other Spiritual Treasures

A Pocket Companion

The Commission on Special Ministries recognizes the ongoing need to lend spiritual support to the men and women who serve their God and country in the military forces of our nation. To that end, we have revised this "Pocket Companion."

We are deeply indebted to the members of The Lutheran Spiritual Welfare Commission, Rev. E. R. Blakewell and Rev. J. G. Jeske, who with the assistance of Professors D. Rohda, E. Schroeder, R. Jungkuntz, R. Gehrke, H. Oswald, and C. Toppe printed the original "Pocket Companion" in 1951. We also acknowledge Pastor Carl Ziemer for his labor of love in revising and updating this helpful booklet.

To all who look to the Triune God for daily strength on their way toward heaven, especially to those on whom burdens lie heavy in peace or in war, we dedicate this little volume.

The WELS Commission on Special Ministries
N16W23377 Stone Ridge Drive
Waukesha, Wisconsin 53188-1108

Revised 2000
Printed 2005, 2012, 2018

Printed in the United States of America

21 22 23 24 25 26 27 28 10 9 8 7 6 5 4 3

Dedication

With this 150th WELS anniversary project, we look back to what we have done in the past, and look toward the future. We anticipate the continued and expanded use of the book. Now it will also be used as a tool in lay ministry for visiting shut-ins, personal and family devotions, and for reaching out to others who have need of God's Word.

We dedicate this book to the many men and women who faithfully serve their God and country. We note especially Mr. Richard Raabe (1923 – 2006), who served his country during World War II, who continued to serve his Lord through his home congregation, and who for 30 years served the Wisconsin Evangelical Lutheran Synod.

TO GOD ALONE BE THE GLORY.

God Our Refuge

FOREWORD

Assurance of heaven and peace of soul are not achieved by doing things for God; rather, they come by trusting in what he has done for us in Jesus, his Son.

This book is intended to help you grasp and hold fast in faith the everlasting blessings that come from the merciful hand of Jesus. *Lord, to whom shall we go? You have the words of eternal life. We believe and know that you are the Holy One of God* (John 6:68-69). *Salvation is found in no one else, for there is no other name under heaven given to men by which we must be saved* (Acts 4:12).

Through him and him alone . . . **God is our Refuge.**

God Our Refuge

Looking to Him

Devotions

Turn to me and be saved,

all you ends of the earth;

for I am God,

and there is no other.

— Isaiah 45:22

Looking to Him

When the Christian looks to his God in time of joy or distress, he needs no special form to express himself. He pours out his inner desires in words born of the moment. Out of the fullness of his heart his tongue speaks freely.

No matter how spontaneous his expression, however, the Christian approaches his Father in heaven in the confidence of faith, clinging to some eternal word of promise. He utters his pleas or his praises, confessing his faith and repeating some blessing that the Lord has pronounced on his children forever. In this natural way he "seeks the Lord" and "calls upon him."

Based on that timeless approach to God, four simple forms are offered for your devotions.

In Any Time or Condition of Life

Devotion

Say:

In the name of the Father and of the Son and of the Holy Ghost. Amen.

Read or repeat from memory some portion of God's eternal Word. Meditate on what the merciful Lord tells you. (Pages 16 to 46 contain a number of short meditations to aid you.)

Then speak your prayers and petitions to God, closing with the Lord's Prayer.

Confess the faith of the whole Christian Church, using the Apostles' Creed.

Conclude:

Lord, bless us and keep us.
Lord, let your face shine on us and be gracious to us.
Lord, look with favor on us and give us peace.
Amen.

In the Morning

Daily Devotion

Early the next morning they arose and worshiped before the LORD . . . — 1 Samuel 1:19

Say:

In the name of the Father and of the Son and of the Holy Spirit.

Then pray:

I thank you, my heavenly Father, through Jesus Christ, your dear Son, that you have kept me this night from all harm and danger. Keep me this day also from sin and every evil, that all my doings and life may please you. Into your hands I commend my body and soul and all things. Let your holy angel be with me, that the wicked foe may have no power over me. Amen.

Read or repeat from memory some portion of God's Word. Meditate on the truth that God speaks to all who read his Word; hold fast the promise and blessing, the admonition and warning which he gives to you this day.

Then confess with the entire Christian church on earth:

I believe in God, the Father almighty, maker of heaven and earth.

I believe in Jesus Christ, his only Son, our Lord, who was conceived by the Holy Spirit, born of the virgin Mary, suffered under Pontius Pilate, was crucified, died, and was buried. He descended into hell. The third day he rose again from the dead. He ascended into heaven and is seated at the right hand of God the Father almighty. From there he will come to judge the living and the dead.

I believe in the Holy Spirit, the holy Christian Church, the communion of saints, the forgiveness of sins, the resurrection of the body, and the life everlasting. Amen.

Then after a hymn or a chief part of Luther's Catechism, go with joy to your work.

In the Evening

Daily Devotion

One of those days Jesus went out to a mountainside to pray, and spent the night praying to God. — Luke 6:12

Say:

In the name of the Father and of the Son and of the Holy Spirit. Amen.

Then pray:

I thank you, my heavenly Father, through Jesus Christ, your dear Son, that you have graciously kept me this day. Forgive me all my sins, and graciously keep me this night. Into your hands I commend my body and soul and all things. Let your holy angel be with me, that the wicked foe may have no power over me. Amen.

Study some chapter of God's Word. Meditate on its meaning for the world in general and for you as a child of God in particular.

Then confess with the whole Christian Church:

I believe in God, the Father almighty, maker of heaven and earth.

I believe in Jesus Christ, his only Son, our Lord, who was conceived by the Holy Spirit, born of the virgin Mary, suffered under Pontius Pilate, was crucified, died, and was buried. He descended into hell. The third day he rose again from the dead. He ascended into heaven and is seated at the right hand of God the Father almighty. From there he will come to judge the living and the dead.

I believe in the Holy Spirit, the holy Christian Church, the communion of saints, the forgiveness of sins, the resurrection of the body, and life everlasting. Amen.

Pray the Lord's Prayer, lie down in peace and sleep.

The Litany

The Litany is a prayer that has been used for centuries in the Christian Church. When the Litany is used in family or group worship, a leader speaks the sentences and the group responds by reading the words in bold type.

O God the Father in heaven,
Have mercy on us.
O God the Son, Redeemer of the world,
Have mercy on us.
O God the Holy Ghost,
Have mercy on us.
Be gracious unto us.
Spare us, good Lord.
From all sin; from all error; from all evil:
Good Lord, deliver us.
O Lord, do not punish us for our sins:
Or reward us according to our iniquities.

Almighty God, our heavenly Father, you do not want any sinner to perish but to turn from his evil way and live. We therefore beg you to spare us the punishment we deserve because of our sins. Forgive our guilt and grant us grace to serve you in holiness and pureness of living; through Jesus Christ, your Son, our Lord. Amen.

In times of tribulation or prosperity, in the hour of death and on the day of judgment:

Help us, good Lord.

To preserve all pastors and ministers of your church in the true knowledge and understanding of your word and in holiness of life; to put an end to all schisms and causes of offense; to beat down Satan under our feet and to comfort and help those who are discouraged and distressed:

Hear us, good Lord.

To grant peace to an undeserving, suffering world, to preserve our country from discord and disaster; to direct and defend our president and all in authority:

Hear us, good Lord.

Our Father who art in heaven; hallowed be thy name, thy kingdom come, thy will be done on earth as it is in heaven. Give us this day our daily bread; and forgive us our trespasses as we forgive those who trespass against us; and lead us not into temptation; But deliver us from evil. For thine is the kingdom and the power and the glory forever and ever. Amen.

God Our Refuge

Seeking Him

Meditations

Seek the LORD while he may be found;

call on him while he is near.

— Isaiah 55:6

IN HIS WORD

Look in the scroll of the LORD and read.
— Isaiah 34:16

Ever since God drove Adam and Eve out of Eden people have looked for God in the most fearful and unusual places—in the shattering lightning, in the devastating earthquake and in the accusing voice of their own conscience. Blinded in sin, people are always hounded by fear and driven by the hopeless desire to somehow escape their own guilt and punishment.

Sinners will never find the true and merciful God in such places, however. He is only to be found where he has made himself known to a fallen world. His ancient prophet Isaiah points out the one place where he has revealed himself to sinners, when he says: *Look in the scroll of the LORD and read.*

There, in his Word, his Holy Scriptures, the Lord God stands in all the fullness of his saving mercy and love. There he stretches out his everlasting arms and bids us: *Come to me . . . and I will give you rest* (Matthew 11:28). For every uneasy, frightening hour of life he extends this promise: *Seek and you will find* (Luke 11:9). *You diligently study the Scriptures because you think that by them you possess eternal life. These are the Scriptures that testify about me* (John 5:39). His Word is *the power of God for the salvation of everyone who believes* (Romans 1:16).

Day after day, when you get up and when you lie down, whether you are in a peaceful home or far away in some strange land, or even out on some shrieking, howling battlefield: *Seek the LORD while he may be found; call on him while he is near* (Isaiah 55:6). *Look in the scroll of the LORD and read*:

Oh, grant that in your holy Word
We here may live and die, dear Lord,
And when our journey ends here,
Receive us into glory there. Amen.

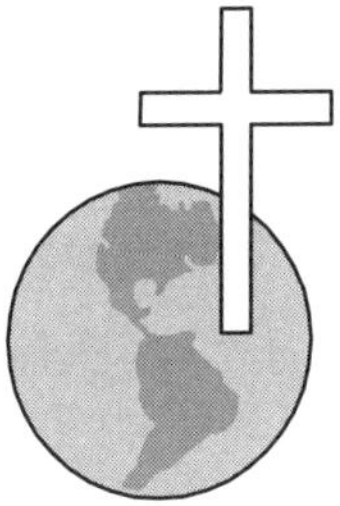

In His Covenant of Baptism

I will make an everlasting covenant with you, my faithful love promised to David. — Isaiah 55:3

Through baptism we are God's children, heirs of God and Christ. *For all of you who were baptized into Christ have clothed yourselves with Christ* (Galatians 3:27). Through baptism our Lord adopts us as his own dear children and gives us his name. His name includes all that he is and stands for: his life, his death, his resurrection, his entire work of salvation—forgiveness of sins, deliverance from death and the devil, eternal life—all of these blessings become ours through this sacrament. That is God's promise and covenant!

Nor are these benefits only temporarily ours. Because God's covenant is everlasting, so are his blessings. Baptism, like the gospel, is an ever-powerful means of grace. We may daily take refuge in our baptism. There our gracious Father provides his children with spiritual strength and comfort.

The devil is devious. The world is full of snares. Our sinful flesh lusts after that which God has forbidden. This ungodly trinity poses a constant and deadly threat to our souls. Our resistance to these cunning, powerful foes dare not be feeble. We dare not grow weary in doing battle. For strength we turn to our baptism. In it we were born again. That new spiritual life is evidence of our victory in Christ. Although our spiritual enemies still tempt us, they have been defeated! When we remember our baptism God provides us with new vigor. Although we often grow weary in our daily struggles, God revives our hearts.

When the day's battle is done, when we have fought our best, we must admit we have fallen far short of what our Lord expects of us. Yes, our lives are full of sin. It is then, when our old Adam would have us believe that God will reject us because of our sin, that we boldly remember our baptism. I am baptized! God himself has washed away my sin and forgiven me. God has promised; he will not break his covenant!

"Though the mountains be shaken and the hills be removed, yet my unfailing love for you will not be shaken nor my covenant of peace be removed," says the LORD, who has compassion on you (Isaiah 54:10). Amen!

In the Gift of the Body and Blood of Our Lord

Whoever eats my flesh and drinks my blood remains in me, and I in him. — John 6:56

Eternal in the heavens, the Lord God omnipotent reigns. He asks counsel of no one, nor must he give answer to any. In his merciful dealings with mankind he chooses his own means of blessing. Whether it appears reasonable to people or not, Jesus says: *Whoever eats my flesh and drinks my blood remains in me, and I in him.*

At one of the darkest moments of their history, God's ancient people were saved by the blood of a lamb. God directed them to paint the blood of a slaughtered lamb on their doorposts. It served as the sign for the angel of death to pass over that home. When the Israelites obeyed their Lord, he spared their firstborn. Though God's choice may have seemed strange and unreasonable, it proved to be right and effective.

God's choice of a means to salvation for us, his New Testament people, also seems strange and unreasonable. God has made it unmistakably clear that the body and the blood of his own Son Jesus is the one sacrifice that can atone for our sins and affect our redemption. His Son has *appeared once for all at the end of the ages to do away with sin by the sacrifice of himself* (Hebrews 9:26).

In this way, our Lord sanctified us by offering the body of Jesus Christ once for all.

- *He himself bore our sins in his body on the tree . . .* (1 Peter 2:24)
- *For you know that it was not with perishable things . . . but with the precious blood of Christ, a lamb without blemish or defect* (1 Peter 1:18-19)
- *. . . the blood of Jesus, his Son, purifies us from all sin* (1 John 1:7)

Jesus not only sacrificed his body and blood for our redemption; he actually gives us that body to eat and that blood to drink in his own Holy Supper. With this crowning gift of his grace and love our Savior binds his people to himself and to one another.

Whenever we Christians are able, therefore, we will receive the blessed gift of his body and blood in his Holy Communion. And although circumstances may occasionally arise which temporarily keep us from partaking of its blessing, our trust in that body and blood will continue to burn within us, a living fire, unto life everlasting. Amen.

In Health

As long as it is day, we must do the work of him who sent me. Night is coming, when no one can work. — John 9:4

"If God brings me through this, if he lets me get better and regain my health, I'll live differently. I'll never neglect him and his church again! Ever!"

Such words may express an honest resolve, but why does our health have to be shattered or threatened before we are willing to make such a good resolve? Wouldn't it be better to concern ourselves about the really important things in life, to *seek first God's kingdom and his righteousness* (Mathew 6:33) while we enjoy the strength and beauty of our youth?

Our Lord Jesus was keenly aware of his heavenly Father's will throughout his earthly life. And yes, he lived accordingly. Surely he serves as an example for us. God has given us a purpose and mission in life as well. He grants us one day after another so that we might boldly proclaim his gospel and courageously carry forward the work of his church. Time is slipping away. Like our Savior, determine to *work while it is day before the night comes when no one can work* (John 9:4).

In plain words, while God is granting you strength, health and opportunity, serve him gladly. Don't wait for illness or accident to bring you to a spiritual crisis. Commit yourself to work for God with holy resolve and true dedication. Heed the invitation of the Apostle Paul who said: *Therefore, I urge you, brothers, in view of God's mercy, to offer your bodies as living sacrifices, holy and pleasing to God—this is your spiritual act of worship* (Romans 12:1).

If one thinks about it for a moment, it most certainly makes sense. In spite of its amazing achievements in our generation, modern science still cannot guarantee or control our health. It remains one of God's most special and wonderful blessings. So while our Lord grants you good health, use it to serve and honor him! Let this be our daily prayer:

Take my life and let it be
Consecrated, Lord to thee.
Take my moments and my days;
Let them flow in ceaseless praise.

Take my love, my Lord, I pour
At thy feet its treasure store.
Take myself, and I will be
Ever, only, all for thee. Amen
(#469 Christian Worship Vs 1,6)

In Sickness

So the sisters sent word to Jesus, "Lord, the one you love is sick." When he heard this, Jesus said, "This sickness will not end in death. No, it is for God's glory so that God's Son may be glorified through it." — John 11:3-4

A cloud of heart-rending gloom hovers over a Christian family in Bethany. Death, defying all medical skill, is stalking Lazarus, the sick brother of Mary and Martha. His strength is failing fast.

Anxious thoughts cross the minds of the sisters in those faith-trying hours. "Why must death take him who is so dear to us? Would that Jesus were here to speak the healing word! Alas, he is far away beyond Jordan!"

Faith surmounts the anguish of the hour by clinging to its firm anchor and hastily dispatching the message to Jesus: *Lord, the one you love is sick.* Hoping that Jesus will restore their brother to health but confessing that their unworthiness doesn't deserve consideration, the sisters simply state their need and appeal to Jesus' love. In humble submission they trust that his wisdom will do what is best.

Jesus' reply comes quickly: *This sickness will not end in death. No, it is for God's glory so that God's Son may be glorified through it.* To that promise and double assurance the sisters and Lazarus are to cling in patient faith and hope as life slowly ebbs away and death settles on his brow.

Four days later, when Jesus' mighty *Come out!* calls Lazarus back to life, he and his sisters experience the marvelous fulfillment of his promise with overwhelming joy. Now they understand the purpose for his sickness and the full import of the words *for the glory of God,* for in raising Lazarus Jesus stands fully revealed as the Resurrection and the Life. His glory was enhanced more by this miracle than if he had only healed Lazarus.

In sickness go to Jesus. His love is ever ready to listen to the prayer of weakest faith and to hear the faintest bleat of his lamb. Cast yourself upon his mercy. Then, like the Bethany family, anchor your faith in his promises and patiently await his answer.

If the death of a loved one is your cross, remember that the golden ray of Christ's promise still shines upon its somber shadow: *Our friend Lazarus has fallen asleep; but I am going there to wake him up* (John 11:11). Amen.

In Worry and Want

So do not worry, saying, "What shall we eat?" or "What shall we drink?" or "What shall we wear?" . . . But seek first his kingdom and his righteousness, and all these things will be given to you as well.
— Matthew 6:31,33

When you are worrying about food and clothing for yourself and your family, prayerfully read Matthew 6:25-34, and see how needless your cares are.

God points you to the green grass, the beautiful flowers and the happy birds. Creatures of little worth, all of them, yet God cares for them. Are you not more precious to God than they? You are God's highest creature. You he created in his own image. Through Christ you are God's dear child and he is your Father. A father is anxious to help his child and delights in providing for him or her. If the Creator already daily provides for the insignificant birds, will the loving Father permit you, his child, to go hungry and unclothed? Will the Father, *who did not spare his own Son, but gave him up for us all—how will he not also, along with him, graciously give us all things* (Romans 8:32)?

God is your heavenly Father. Heaven and earth and all their store are his. He has an abundance from which to supply your want. He rules over all. His strong arm is able to give you what you need. *Your heavenly Father knows that you need all these things* (Matthew 6:32). His wisdom knows what to supply and how much is best for us. Can we ask for more? Small wonder that he addresses us who are prone to worry about earthly things: *O you of little faith* (Matthew 6:30)! By not trusting him to take care of our earthly needs we become like the heathen who do not know or trust their Father in heaven.

If our heavenly Father is withholding from us the full measure of earthly gifts that we desire for our comfort, he is really giving us a blessing in disguise. Thereby he teaches us to cast all our cares upon him and helps us to get away from things earthly and to learn that these are not of the first importance. To believe and trust in him is to be our chief concern. Amen.

Seek first his kingdom and his righteousness, and all these things will be given to you as well. — Matthew 6:33

In Prosperity

. . . when you eat and are satisfied, be careful that you do not forget the LORD . . .

— Deuteronomy 6:11-12

Days of prosperity are often more dangerous than days of scarcity and need. The earthly blessings of prosperous days have a way of crowding God and the things of heaven out of our thoughts and lives. That is why God warned his Old Testament people as he was about to bless them with the promised land of plenty . . . *when you eat and are satisfied, be careful that you do not forget the LORD . . .*

The sin of forgetting the Lord goes straight back to the garden of Eden. Adam forgot his loving Creator. He failed to love his Lord more than anything else. And yes, he failed to trust in him as the one who had blessed him with all things. Ingratitude and unbelief led him to disobey his God. For us American Christians, full-blooded sons of sinful Adam, who have a land more richly blessed by God than any other, surely there is great need that God daily remind each of us: *. . . when you eat and are satisfied, be careful that you do not forget the LORD . . .*

With every new day of prosperity we should earnestly remember that God has not placed us in this world to achieve earthly honor, pile up earthly wealth, and gain earthly luxuries and ease. On the contrary: *Our citizenship is in heaven* (Philippians 3:20). For that reason our Lord also has told us, *Do not store up for yourselves treasures on earth, where moth and rust destroy, and where thieves break in and steal (Matthew 6:19).* Instead, set your affections on things above.

In our materialistic generation which has pros- pered so much at the horrible cost of war and wholesale bloodshed, we should pray as never before that God teach us to appreciate all the earthly blessings he gives us, but hang our hearts on none.

The rich fool, forgetful of God, laid his own plans and was well on his way to carry them out (read Luke 12:16-21), when God suddenly stopped him in his tracks. *God said to him: "You fool! This very night your life will be demanded from you. Then who will get what you have prepared for yourself"* (Luke 12:20)?

In prosperity, O Lord, keep me from the way of the fool; keep me humble and faithful so that I may never forget or forsake you! Amen.

In Ever-Present Temptation

Therefore put on the full armor of God, so that when the day of evil comes, you may be able to stand your ground, and after you have done everything, to stand. — Ephesians 6:13

Temptation lines the full length of life's way for every one of us. The reason for it is perfectly clear: *God tempts no one but each one is tempted when, by his own evil desire, he is dragged away and enticed* (James 1:13-14). Thus, those ever-present tempta- tions that assail us have their origin in our own sinful flesh, in the devil and in the world. And sadly, our sinful nature is always ready to cooperate with this wicked trinity!

It is evident, therefore, that in our struggle against temptation the odds are definitely against us. *Our struggle is not against flesh and blood, but against the rulers, against the authorities, against the powers of this dark world and against the spiritual forces of evil in the heavenly realms* (Ephesians 6:12).

We simply do not possess the power to conquer such formidable foes. As often as we feel that we are strong enough to cope with them and conquer, we find, as did Peter in the courtyard of the high priest's palace, that the tempter and the forces of evil have woefully overpowered and brought us down in sin and denial.

There is, however, still a way by which every one of us can conquer in spite of our own sins and weakness.

St. Paul outlines the way to victory over every temptation in his letter to the Ephesians. Surely, we can do nothing better than to carve his words on our memory forever:

> *Therefore put on the full armor of God, so that when the day of evil comes, you may be able to stand your ground, and after you have done everything, to stand. Stand firm then, with the belt of truth buckled around your waist, with the breastplate of righteousness in place, with your feet fitted with the readiness that comes from the gospel of peace. In addition to all this, take up the shield of faith, with which you can extinguish all the flaming arrows of the evil one. Take the helmet of salvation and the sword of the Spirit, which is the word of God* (Ephesians 6:13-17).

There, my friend, lies the only way to victory when tempted. Follow it and conquer by the power of God. Amen.

In Sorrow

Jesus replied, " . . . later you will understand."
— John 13:7

It is when the human heart finds itself floundering in sorrow that it cries out its bewildered, lamenting "*Why?*" "*Why* did my only son have to fall thousands of miles from home on that shell-torn battlefield?" "If science can explode the atom, *why* couldn't it save my baby?" "*Why* did my husband have to . . . ?" "*Why* did my wife . . . ?" "*Why . . . why?*"

Only Christians can find a satisfying, comforting answer to that human, never dying "*why?*" For as the Christian looks in trust and hope to Christ his Lord, he finds him giving that answer in an hour when his own soul was *overwhelmed with sorrow to the point of death he said to them, "Stay here and keep watch"* (Mark 14:34).

In his last night on earth Jesus did things which his disciples could not understand. They were therefore asking themselves: "Why? Why was he washing their feet? Why was he speaking of leaving them? Why?" Jesus knew it. And, echoing the faith and conviction that bound him to his heavenly Father in every hour of his own sorrow, he told them: *You do not realize now what I am doing, but later you will understand* (John 13:7).

It meant: "I know what I am doing, and I am doing it in order to bring you blessings. You may not understand now, but you will understand later—if not in this life, then in the life to come."

Such was the confidence in Jesus' own heart toward his Father in heaven—that confidence which in Gethsemane enabled him in the midst of agony and anguish to pray, *Father, . . . not my will but yours be done* (Luke 22:42). This is the confidence that will bind us in trust to God and his Christ in every heavy hour of life.

In the depths of your sorrow, when your heart is tempted to cry out its lamenting "Why?" grasp the hand of Jesus your Lord in simple faith and listen to him tell you: "I know the reason and in mercy have measured the purpose of your sorrow. Trust me now, and . . . *later you will understand.*"

If our soul can find no comfort,
If despondency grows strong,
And the heart cries out in anguish:
"O my God, how long, how long?"
Comfort then our aching breast,
Grant it courage, patience, rest. Amen.

In Trial

My son, do not despise the Lord's discipline and do not resent his rebuke, because the LORD disciplines those he loves, as a father the son he delights in. — Proverbs 3:11-12

Trials sometimes come fast and furious for the Christian. Afflictions, wave upon wave, dashed against Job, a man *blameless and upright* (Job 1:1). Lightning struck and all his cattle became charred carcasses. The Arabs seized all his property. A tornado shattered the house of his oldest son and Job's ten children lay dead in its twisted ruins. Painful sores racked his body and a loathsome disease sapped its strength. Friends left him comfortless. His own wife laughed him to scorn for trusting in God.

Amid all those fiery trials Job confessed: *The Lord gave, and the Lord has taken away* (Job 1:21). My present trouble, whatever it may be, is mine not by chance or accident. It comes to me from the Lord. He does not want me to regard it lightly or to despise it; rather, he wants me to be quick to recognize his good and wise purpose in sending it.

My present trial is not a punishment of a stern, angry God. By it he intends to chasten and correct me. Love, not hatred, prompts a father to correct his child. With his correcting hand he wants to help the child grow up into a strong Christian character. In the same way my heavenly Father is testing, purifying and strengthening my faith in the furnace of affliction. Through tribulations he wants to draw me closer to himself and in the end save my soul.

When the burdens of life press down heavily upon you, when your flesh finds these corrections irksome and your spirit grows weary and begins to complain, look to Jesus for guidance, patience and an understanding heart. Consider how patiently he endured all *for the joy that was set before him.* He has told us, *My yoke is easy, and my burden is light* (Matthew 11:13). Scripture promises that . . . *when you are tempted, he (God) will also provide a way out so that you can stand up under it* (1 Corinthians 10:13). Amen.

Be still, my soul; the Lord is on your side;
Bear patiently the cross of grief or pain;
Leave to your God to order and provide;
In ev'ry change he faithful will remain.
Be still, my soul; your best, your heav'nly friend
Through thorny ways leads to a joyful end.
(#415 Christian Worship Vs. 1)

In Spiritual Doubt

When John heard in prison what Christ was doing, he sent his disciples to ask him, "Are you the one who was to come, or should we expect someone else?" — Matthew 11:2-3

Our most soul-shaking hours are the hours of spiritual doubt. When the Christian heart trembles and asks, "Does Christ really care? Is he really God's Son, really the world's Redeemer, my Savior and Lord?"—earth threatens to lose every gleam of hope and eternity threatens to black out in cold despair. What shall you and I do in such times of hellish, questioning doubt?

John the Baptist, the peerless herald of Jesus, gives us the most effective answer. When John lay bound in Herod's prison-fortress and Jesus did not personally come to him, it seems that this dark question arose within him. Was Jesus the Christ that should come, the one he thought he was—or should he bid God's people look for another? John recog-nized in that question a danger that might shatter his faith and wreck his soul.

There was only one way to conquer and that was to seek an answer from the Lord about whom doubt was rising. John therefore sent two of his disciples straight to Jesus, asking: *Are you the one who was to come, or should we expect someone else* (Luke 7:19)?

Jesus replied as only the merciful Savior could. He did not answer John's question directly, but sent back to John clear and undeniable evidence that he was indeed *the one who was to come*. When Jesus spoke in answer John the Baptist regained his confidence. His doubts were forever gone.

When doubts arise in you to threaten your soul's salvation, follow John straight to Jesus himself. Go into his Word and there let him answer for himself. See him there as the God-sent Redeemer of mankind, healing the blind, the deaf, and the crippled; cleansing the lepers; raising the dead; and above all preaching the gospel to hopeless, trembling sinners. Then your doubts too will be silenced. As did John, you too will see Jesus as the Christ of God, the Redeemer of the world, your own Savior and Lord. You too will understand fully then what he meant when he said: *Blessed is the man who does not fall away on account of me* (Matthew 11:6). Amen.

I wait for the Lord
and in his Word I put my hope. — Psalm 130:5

In Time of Peril for the Church

And I tell you that you are Peter, and on this rock I will build my church, and the gates of Hades will not overcome it. — Matthew 16:18

To create and nourish saving faith, our Lord gave believers his precious Word and the Holy Sacraments. Those who believe in Jesus as their Savior make up his holy Christian church. By grace he has made you and me a member of that church.

This church, dearer to me than wife and child, is exposed to constant peril. Ruthless attacks against her by outspoken, unscrupulous foes—vain attempts to build her with other than spiritual material by those who sincerely claim membership—even I, sometimes indifferent and unappreciative of her blessings, oppress and distress her.

Exposed to attacks from without and failings from within, at times her very existence seems threatened. Even pious Elijah, detecting no signs of her presence, complained: *I am the only one left* (1 Kings 19:10). Zion, Israel's faithful remnant—captive, her holy city destroyed, her temple in ruins—like a lonely bride imagining that the love of her groom has cooled, tearfully laments: *The Lord has forsaken me, the Lord has forgotten me* (Isaiah 49:14). In words of tenderest affection the Bridegroom assures his church of his everlasting love: *Can a mother forget the baby at her breast and have no compassion on the child she has borne? Though she may forget, I will not forget you* (Isaiah 49:15)! In similar manner the Lord assured Elijah that seven thousand had not bowed to Baal. God's church of believers had not perished!

If you are not giving your best in church work because you imagine your energy is being spent for a hopeless cause, if you fear that the church will not survive, then remember the farewell promise that the triumphantly ascending Jesus—the head, builder and cornerstone—gave her: *Surely, I am with you always, to the very end of the age* (Matthew 28:20). For the benefit of the church God the Father *has put everything under his (Jesus') feet* (1 Corinthians 15:27). All enemies will be made his footstool. Upon the last enemy to encompass the camp of the saints on Judgment Day he will drop fire *down from heaven* (Revelation 20:9). He promises to shorten those last days of tribulation for the church's sake. We confidently trust that the church in conflict will become the church in glory, for against her *the gates of Hades will not overcome it.* Amen.

IN TIME OF NATIONAL DANGER

When men tell you to consult mediums and spiritists, who whisper and mutter, should not a people inquire of their God? Why consult the dead on behalf of the living? — Isaiah 8:19

When the nation we love is in danger, what should we do to help ward off disaster? There is something even more important than strengthening her physical defenses and building a strong morale within her, for *unless the Lord builds the house, its builders labor in vain* (Psalm 127:1). Thus, the most important thing a Christian can do for his nation in danger is indicated in those challenging words of the Scripture: *. . . should not a people inquire of their God?*

We must not forget that God Almighty is still in complete control. This is true even at a time when people consider themselves the masters of their own future, enlisting the very inner forces of nature to guarantee that future. It is the Lord who sets history's stage for the future and prepares nations and peoples for rise or for fall. History reveals many an instance where unbelieving leaders were confidently preparing their nation for a brilliant and powerful future, when suddenly the Almighty set their course in the opposite direction.

Remember, God's all-powerful arm has not been shortened even today. He will do whatever he determines according to his wisdom and might. With him rest the issues of prosperity or trouble for even the mightiest and most promising of nations. Surrounded by a God-forgetting generation, we Christians can do no better than to confidently pray to our God on our nation's behalf.

Do it! Pray that God would make our people repentant and faithful. Pray that he would give us wise and able leaders, that he would replace our weaknesses of today with strength for tomorrow; that he would bless our military and nation whenever and wherever it encounters enemies. And when we enjoy peace and prosperity, pray that God would keep us humble and upright. This is the greatest service we can do for the nation we love so dearly. A nation whose Christians seek out their God for blessing is a nation that God will not forget!

Our God, our help in ages past,
Our hope for years to come,
Still be our guard while troubles last
And our eternal home!
(#441 Christian Worship Vs. 6)

In the Fear of Death

Even though I walk through the valley of the shadow of death, I will fear no evil, for you are with me; your rod and your staff, they comfort me.

— Psalm 23:4

Death threatens the sheep as their shepherd leads them through one of the valleys of Palestine. The valleys are deep and rugged with sharp stones scattered everywhere. They are also forbidding to the sheep because of the thieves and wolves that lie in wait for them along its dense, dark ravines.

But the shepherd knows the frail and fearful nature of his timid sheep. He carries two weapons for their protection. With his staff he strikes the poisonous snakes that threaten the flock. He rescues young lambs caught in the thicket by hooking them with its crook. His rod, a short club with a ball of iron for the hand to grasp at one end and a larger knob of metal with spiked nails at the other, he hurls at the attacking wolf with deadly accuracy. As he walks along, he strikes the iron rod against the hard stone cliffs. The hillsides re-echo the ringing sound that frightens away lurking enemies. Above it all, the sheep hear the shepherd's own distinctive call reassuring them that he is leading and protecting them.

Everyone must pass through death's dread valley because of sin. Even Christians cannot escape it. But in passing through it they need fear no evil. Christ, our Good Shepherd, knows our needs in death's hour and is with us. When we become fearful, he lets his gracious voice be heard. His gospel promises ring out a clear note reassuring us that he is on the lookout. With Jesus in the lead we know the destination that he has in view. We enter the valley of the shadow of death knowing that it is but the gateway to life.

Even though death, like the shadow, is only a few steps ahead of me, even though I am in the very jaws and grip of death, I fear no evil. With his death Christ has overcome death for me. He will keep me safe. No, not even death can pluck me out of his hand! Jesus promised. Amen.

Be merciful to me, LORD, for I am faint;
O LORD, heal me, for . . . my soul is in anguish.

Turn, O LORD, and deliver me;
Save me because of your unfailing love.
— Psalm 6:2

In the Face of Eternity

For my Father's will is that everyone who looks to the Son and believes in him shall have eternal life, and I will raise him up at the last day.

— John 6:40

Man is destined to die once, and after that to face judgment. Those solemn words of God's Scripture, written in Hebrews 9:27, remind us of the inescapable hour when time must end and eternity must begin for every one of us.

Even in us Christians—men and women of little faith that we are—the sinful human heart beats uneasily at the thought of death and eternity. There is but one thing that can actually enable us to stand confident and unafraid in the face of eternity. It is the assurance of Jesus our Savior that in his mercy he has taken pity on us and in his grace has gained for us pardon and blessing for all eternity. Such assurance he has given us in abundance.

> *Whoever hears my word and believes him who sent me has eternal life and will not be condemned; he has crossed over from death to life* (John 5:24). *For the Son of Man came to seek and to save what was lost* (Luke 19:10). *For my father's will is that everyone who looks to the Son*

and believes in him shall have eternal life, and I will raise him at the last day (John 6:40).

In those and many other words like them Christ, our Redeemer-Lord, lights up eternity with heavenly promise and hope.

He does even more. In those words he who conquered death and gave proof of it to the world with his own triumphant rising points us ahead to the great resurrection's glorious morning. Our risen Savior repeats his promise which is so bright with eternal blessing: *I will raise him at the last day.*

With that assurance ringing in your soul you can look ahead, confident in Christ your Lord—even in the face of eternity. On the other side of that thin line that separates time and eternity your risen Lord stands, assuring you: *Because I live, you will also live* (John 14:19). Amen.

My Savior paid the debt I owe
And for my sin was smitten;
Within the Book of Life I know
My name has now been written.
I will not doubt, for I am free,
And Satan cannot threaten me;
There is no condemnation!

God Our Refuge

FINDING HIM

Gospel-Readings

Wherever I cause

my name to be honored,

I will come to you

and bless you.

— Exodus 20:24

MARTIN LUTHER'S COAT OF ARMS

The Heart of the Gospel

The word "gospel" means good news. News always implies that an event has taken place. The Christian gospel is not merely a system of religious teachings or a set of rules for moral conduct. The unique and essential aspect of Christianity is that it depends entirely upon an event, namely, the entry of God himself into human history in the person of his Son, Jesus Christ. This characteristic distinguishes our faith from all others.

When God became human, something happened which changed the whole meaning of mankind's existence from Adam on. The Bible speaks of this change under various terms: redemption, reconciliation, justification, salvation. Most important is the fact that this change was wrought through the event of one person's coming into the world, through the birth, life, death, resurrection and ascension of Jesus of Nazareth.

This truth prompted the early church to call each of the first four books of the New Testament gospels, the Gospel—according to Matthew, Mark, Luke, and John, respectively. By inspiration of the Holy Spirit, each of these writers has set down the story of that great event, the saving act of God in his Son who became fully human.

The following pages contain, in the words of the evangelists themselves, the *heart* of this gospel. Unquestionably, some omitted portions of the sacred narrative are fully as meaningful and important as certain of the selections included here; yet, a choice had to be made. In making a choice, the editors' only endeavor was to offer in brief scope as much of the gospel as possible.

Boldface type has been used to set off brief passages which through long familiarity are especially dear to us, or which state a divine truth in particularly memorable words. Instead of the usual verse divisions, paragraphs have been used to encourage the reading of God's Word as a connected whole. That is how it should be read; for it is the good news, the gospel, the story of the most important event that ever took place.

The Incarnation

John 1:1-14

In the beginning was the Word, and the Word was with God, and the Word was God. He was with God in the beginning.

Through him all things were made; without him nothing was made that has been made. In him was life, and that life was the light of men. The light shines in the darkness, but the darkness has not understood it.

There came a man who was sent from God; his name was John. He came as a witness to testify concerning that light, so that through him all men might believe. He himself was not the light; he came only as a witness to the light. The true light that gives light to every man was coming into the world.

He was in the world, and though the world was made through him, the world did not recognize him. He came to that which was his own, but his own did not receive him. Yet to all who received him, to those who believed in his name, he gave the right to become children of God—children born not of natural descent, nor of human decision or a husband's will, but born of God.

The Word became flesh and made his dwelling among us. We have seen his glory, the glory of the One and Only, who came from the Father, full of grace and truth.

Matthew 1:18-25

This is how the birth of Jesus Christ came about: His mother Mary was pledged to be married to Joseph, but before they came together, she was found to be with child through the Holy Spirit. Because Joseph her husband was a righteous man and did not want to expose her to public disgrace, he had in mind to divorce her quietly.

But after he had considered this, an angel of the Lord appeared to him in a dream and said, "Joseph son of David, do not be afraid to take Mary home as your wife, because what is conceived in her is from the Holy Spirit. She will give birth to a son, and you are to give him the name Jesus, because he will save his people from their sins."

All this took place to fulfill what the Lord had said through the prophet: "The virgin will be with child and will give birth to a son, and they will call him Immanuel"—which means, "God with us."

When Joseph woke up, he did what the angel of the Lord had commanded him and took Mary home as his wife. But he had no union with her until she gave birth to a son. And he gave him the name Jesus.

Luke 2:1-14

In those days Caesar Augustus issued a decree that a census should be taken of the entire Roman world. (This was the first census that took place while Quirinius was governor of Syria.) And everyone went to his own town to register.

So Joseph also went up from the town of Nazareth in Galilee to Judea, to Bethlehem the town of David, because he belonged to the house and line of David. He went there to register with Mary, who was pledged to be married to him and was expecting a child. While they were there, the time came for the baby to be born, and she gave birth to her firstborn, a son. She wrapped him in cloths and placed him in a manger, because there was no room for them in the inn.

And there were shepherds living out in the fields nearby, keeping watch over their flocks at night. An angel of the Lord appeared to them, and the glory of the Lord shone around them, and they were terrified. But the angel said to them, "Do not be afraid. I bring you good news of great joy that will be for all the people. **Today in the town of David a Savior has been born to you; he is Christ the Lord.** This will be a sign to you: You will find a baby wrapped in cloths and lying in a manger."

Suddenly a great company of the heavenly host appeared with the angel, praising God and saying, "Glory to God in the highest, and on earth peace to men on whom his favor rests."

The Baptism of Jesus

Matthew 3:1-17

In those days John the Baptist came, preaching in the Desert of Judea and saying, "Repent, for the kingdom of heaven is near." This is he who was spoken of through the prophet Isaiah: "A voice of one calling in the desert, 'Prepare the way for the Lord, make straight paths for him.'"

John's clothes were made of camel's hair, and he had a leather belt around his waist. His food was locusts and wild honey. People went out to him from Jerusalem and all Judea and the whole region of the Jordan. Confessing their sins, they were baptized by him in the Jordan River.

But when he saw many of the Pharisees and Sadducees coming to where he was baptizing, he said to them: "You brood of vipers! Who warned you to flee from the coming wrath? Produce fruit in keeping with repentance. And do not think you can say to yourselves, 'We have Abraham as our father.' I tell you that out of these stones God can raise up children for Abraham. The ax is already at the root of the trees, and every tree that does not produce good fruit will be cut down and thrown into the fire.

"I baptize you with water for repentance. But after me will come one who is more powerful than I, whose sandals I am not fit to carry. He will baptize you with the Holy Spirit and with fire. His winnowing fork is in his hand, and he will clear his threshing floor, gathering his wheat into the barn and burning up the chaff with unquenchable fire."

Then Jesus came from Galilee to the Jordan to be baptized by John. But John tried to deter him, saying, "I need to be baptized by you, and do you come to me?"

Jesus replied, "Let it be so now; it is proper for us to do this to fulfill all righteousness." Then John consented.

As soon as Jesus was baptized, he went up out of the water. At that moment heaven was opened, and he saw the Spirit of God descending like a dove and lighting on him. And a voice from heaven said, "This is my Son, whom I love; with him I am well pleased."

THE TEMPTATION

Matthew 4:1-11

Then Jesus was led by the Spirit into the desert to be tempted by the devil. After fasting forty days and forty nights, he was hungry. The tempter came to him and said, "If you are the Son of God, tell these stones to become bread."

Jesus answered, "It is written: 'Man does not live on bread alone, but on every word that comes from the mouth of God.'"

Then the devil took him to the holy city and had him stand on the highest point of the temple. "If you are the Son of God," he said, "throw yourself down. For it is written: 'He will command his angels concerning you, and they will lift you up in their hands, so that you will not strike your foot against a stone.'" Jesus answered him, "It is also written: 'Do not put the Lord your God to the test.'"

Again, the devil took him to a very high mountain and showed him all the kingdoms of the world and their splendor. "All this I will give you," he said, "if you will bow down and worship me."

Jesus said to him, "Away from me, Satan! For it is written: 'Worship the Lord your God, and serve him only.'"

Then the devil left him, and angels came and attended him.

JESUS AND NICODEMUS

John 3:1-16

Now there was a man of the Pharisees named Nicodemus, a member of the Jewish ruling council. He came to Jesus at night and said, "Rabbi, we know you are a teacher who has come from God. For no one could perform the miraculous signs you are doing if God were not with him."

In reply Jesus declared, "I tell you the truth, no one can see the kingdom of God unless he is born again."

"How can a man be born when he is old?" Nicodemus asked. "Surely he cannot enter a second time into his mother's womb to be born!"

Jesus answered, **"I tell you the truth, no one can enter the kingdom of God unless he is born of water and the Spirit.** Flesh gives birth to flesh, but the Spirit gives birth to spirit. You should not be surprised at my saying, 'You must be born again.' The wind blows wherever it pleases. You hear its sound, but you cannot tell where it comes from or where it is going. So it is with everyone born of the Spirit."

"How can this be?" Nicodemus asked.

"You are Israel's teacher," said Jesus, "and do you not understand these things? I tell you the truth, we speak of what we know, and we testify to what we have seen, but still you people do not accept our testimony. I have spoken to you of earthly things and you do not believe; how then will you believe if I speak of heavenly things? No one has ever gone into heaven except the one who came from heaven—the Son of Man. **Just as Moses lifted up the snake in the desert, so the Son of Man must be lifted up, that everyone who believes in him may have eternal life. For God so loved the world that he gave his one and only Son, that whoever believes in him shall not perish but have eternal life."**

The Sermon on the Mount

Matthew 5:1-16

Now when he saw the crowds, he went up on a mountainside and sat down. His disciples came to him, and he began to teach them, saying:

"Blessed are the poor in spirit, for theirs is the kingdom of heaven.
Blessed are those who mourn, for they will be comforted.
Blessed are the meek, for they will inherit the earth.

"Blessed are those who hunger and thirst for righteousness, for they will be filled.
Blessed are the merciful, for they will be shown mercy.
Blessed are the pure in heart, for they will see God.
Blessed are the peacemakers, for they will be called sons of God.
Blessed are those who are persecuted because of righteousness, for theirs is the kingdom of heaven.

"Blessed are you when people insult you, persecute you and falsely say all kinds of evil against you because of me. Rejoice and be glad, because great is your reward in heaven, for in the same way they persecuted the prophets who were before you.

"**You are the salt of the earth.** But if the salt loses its saltiness, how can it be made salty again? It is no longer good for anything, except to be thrown out and trampled by men.

"**You are the light of the world.** A city on a hill cannot be hidden. Neither do people light a lamp and put it under a bowl. Instead they put it on its stand, and it gives light to everyone in the house. In the same way, let your light shine before men, that they may see your good deeds and praise your Father in heaven."

Matthew 6:25-33

"Therefore I tell you, do not worry about your life, what you will eat or drink; or about your body, what you will wear. Is not life more important than food, and the body more important than clothes? **Look at the birds of the air; they do not sow or reap or store away in barns, and yet your heavenly Father feeds them. Are you not much more valuable than they?** Who of you by worrying can add a single hour to his life?

"And why do you worry about clothes? See how the lilies of the field grow. They do not labor or spin. Yet I tell you that not even Solomon in all his splendor was dressed like one of these. If that is how God clothes the grass of the field, which is here today and tomorrow is thrown into the fire, will he not much more clothe you, O you of little faith?

"So do not worry, saying, 'What shall we eat?' or 'What shall we drink?' or 'What shall we wear?' For the pagans run after all these things, and your heavenly Father knows that you need them. But seek first his kingdom and his righteousness, and all these things will be given to you as well."

Matthew 7:7-12

"Ask and it will be given to you; seek and you will find; knock and the door will be opened to you. For everyone who asks receives; he who seeks finds; and to him who knocks, the door will be opened.

"Which of you, if his son asks for bread, will give him a stone? Or if he asks for a fish, will give him a snake? If you, then, though you are evil, know how to give good gifts to your children, how much more will your Father in heaven give good gifts to those who ask him! So in everything, do to others what you would have them do to you, for this sums up the Law and the Prophets."

Blessing the Children

Mark 10:13-16

People were bringing little children to Jesus to have him touch them, but the disciples rebuked them. When Jesus saw this, he was indignant. He said to them, "Let the little children come to me, and do not hinder them, for the kingdom of God belongs to such as these. **I tell you the truth, anyone who will not receive the kingdom of God like a little child will never enter it.**" And he took the children in his arms, put his hands on them and blessed them.

Parables

Luke 15:1-24

The tax collectors and "sinners" were all gathering around to hear him. But the Pharisees and the teachers of the law muttered, "This man welcomes sinners and eats with them."

Then Jesus told them this parable: "Suppose one of you has a hundred sheep and loses one of them. Does he not leave the ninety-nine in the open country and go after the lost sheep until he finds it? And when he finds it, he joyfully puts it on his shoulders and goes home. Then he calls his friends and neighbors together and says, 'Rejoice with me; I have found my lost sheep.' I tell you that in the same way there will be more rejoicing in heaven over one sinner who repents than over ninety-nine righteous persons who do not need to repent.

"Or suppose a woman has ten silver coins and loses one. Does she not light a lamp, sweep the house and search carefully until she finds it? And when she finds it, she calls her friends and neighbors together and says, 'Rejoice with me; I have found my lost coin.' In the same way, I tell you, there is rejoicing in the presence of the angels of God over one sinner who repents."

Jesus continued: "There was a man who had two sons. The younger one said to his father, 'Father, give me my share of the estate.' So he divided his property between them.

"Not long after that, the younger son got together all he had, set off for a distant country and there squandered his wealth in wild living. After he had spent everything, there was a severe famine in that whole country, and he began to be in need. So he went and hired himself out to a citizen of that country, who sent him to his fields to feed pigs. He longed to fill his stomach with the pods that the pigs were eating, but no one gave him anything.

"When he came to his senses, he said, 'How many of my father's hired men have food to spare, and here I am starving to death! I will set out and go back to my father and say to him: Father, I have sinned against heaven and against you. I am no longer worthy to be called your son; make me like one of your hired men.' So he got up and went to his father.

"But while he was still a long way off, his father saw him and was filled with compassion for him; he ran to his son, threw his arms around him and kissed him.

"The son said to him, 'Father, I have sinned against heaven and against you. I am no longer worthy to be called your son.'

"But the father said to his servants, 'Quick! Bring the best robe and put it on him. Put a ring on his finger and sandals on his feet. Bring the fattened calf and kill it. Let's have a feast and celebrate. For this son of mine was dead and is alive again; he was lost and is found.' So they began to celebrate."

The Raising of Lazarus

John 11:1-27, 32-45

Now a man named Lazarus was sick. He was from Bethany, the village of Mary and her sister Martha. This Mary, whose brother Lazarus now lay sick, was the same one who poured perfume on the Lord and wiped his feet with her hair. So the sisters sent word to Jesus, "Lord, the one you love is sick."

When he heard this, Jesus said, "This sickness will not end in death. No, it is for God's glory so that God's Son may be glorified through it." Jesus loved Martha and her sister and Lazarus. Yet when he heard that Lazarus was sick, he stayed where he was two more days.

Then he said to his disciples, "Let us go back to Judea." "But Rabbi," they said, "a short while ago the Jews tried to stone you, and yet you are going back there?"

Jesus answered, "Are there not twelve hours of daylight? A man who walks by day will not stumble, for he sees by this world's light. It is when he walks by night that he stumbles, for he has no light."

After he had said this, he went on to tell them, "Our friend Lazarus has fallen asleep; but I am going there to wake him up."

His disciples replied, "Lord, if he sleeps, he will get better." Jesus had been speaking of his death, but his disciples thought he meant natural sleep.

So then he told them plainly, "Lazarus is dead, and for your sake I am glad I was not there, so that you may believe. But let us go to him." Then Thomas (called Didymus) said to the rest of the disciples, "Let us also go, that we may die with him."

On his arrival, Jesus found that Lazarus had already been in the tomb for four days. Bethany was less than two miles from Jerusalem, and many Jews had come to Martha and Mary to comfort them in the loss of their brother. When Martha heard that Jesus was coming, she went out to meet him, but Mary stayed at home.

"Lord," Martha said to Jesus, "if you had been here, my brother would not have died. But I know that even now God will give you whatever you ask." Jesus said to her, "Your brother will rise again." Martha answered, "I know he will rise again in the resurrection at the last day."

Jesus said to her, **"I am the resurrection and the life. He who believes in me will live, even though he dies; and whoever lives and believes in me will never die.** Do you believe this?"

"Yes, Lord," she told him, "I believe that you are the Christ, the Son of God, who was to come into the world . . ."

When Mary reached the place where Jesus was and saw him, she fell at his feet and said, "Lord, if you had been here, my brother would not have died."

When Jesus saw her weeping, and the Jews who had come along with her also weeping, he was deeply moved in spirit and troubled. "Where have you laid him?" he asked. "Come and see, Lord," they replied. Jesus wept.

Then the Jews said, "See how he loved him!" But some of them said, "Could not he who opened the eyes of the blind man have kept this man from dying?"

Jesus, once more deeply moved, came to the tomb. It was a cave with a stone laid across the entrance. "Take away the stone," he said.

"But, Lord," said Martha, the sister of the dead man, "by this time there is a bad odor, for he has been there four days." Then Jesus said, "Did I not tell you that if you believed, you would see the glory of God?"

So they took away the stone. Then Jesus looked up and said, "Father, I thank you that you have heard me.

I knew that you always hear me, but I said this for the benefit of the people standing here, that they may believe that you sent me."

When he had said this, Jesus called in a loud voice, "Lazarus, come out!" The dead man came out, his hands and feet wrapped with strips of linen, and a cloth around his face. Jesus said to them, "Take off the grave clothes and let him go."

Therefore many of the Jews who had come to visit Mary, and had seen what Jesus did, put their faith in him.

The Last Discourses

John 14:1-6

"Do not let your hearts be troubled. Trust in God; trust also in me. In my Father's house are many rooms; if it were not so, I would have told you. **I am going there to prepare a place for you. And if I go and prepare a place for you, I will come back and take you to be with me that you also may be where I am.** You know the way to the place where I am going."

Thomas said to him, "Lord, we don't know where you are going, so how can we know the way?"

Jesus answered, **"I am the way and the truth and the life. No one comes to the Father except through me."**

John 14:15-18

"If you love me, you will obey what I command. And I will ask the Father, and **he will give you another Counselor to be with you forever—the Spirit of truth.** The world cannot accept him, because it neither sees him nor knows him. But you know him, for he lives with you and will be in you. I will not leave you as orphans; I will come to you."

John 15:1-5

"I am the true vine, and my Father is the gardener. He cuts off every branch in me that bears no fruit, while every branch that does bear fruit he prunes so that it will be even more fruitful. You are already clean because of the word I have spoken to you. Remain in me, and I will remain in you. No branch can bear fruit by itself; it must remain in the vine. Neither can you bear fruit unless you remain in me.

"I am the vine; you are the branches. If a man remains in me and I in him, he will bear much fruit; apart from me you can do nothing."

THE PASSION

Luke 22:18, 14-23

Now the Feast of Unleavened Bread, called the Passover, was approaching, and the chief priests and the teachers of the law were looking for some way to get rid of Jesus, for they were afraid of the people. Then Satan entered Judas, called Iscariot, one of the Twelve. And Judas went to the chief priests and the officers of the temple guard and discussed with them how he might betray Jesus. They were delighted and agreed to give him money. He consented, and watched for an opportunity to hand Jesus over to them when no crowd was present.

Then came the day of Unleavened Bread on which the Passover lamb had to be sacrificed. Jesus sent Peter and John, saying, "Go and make preparations for us to eat the Passover . . . "

When the hour came, Jesus and his apostles reclined at the table. And he said to them, "I have eagerly desired to eat this Passover with you before I suffer. For I tell you, I will not eat it again until it finds fulfillment in the kingdom of God."

After taking the cup, he gave thanks and said, "Take this and divide it among you. For I tell you I will not drink again of the fruit of the vine until the kingdom of God comes."

And he took bread, gave thanks and broke it, and gave it to them, saying, "This is my body given for you; do this in remembrance of me."

In the same way, after the supper he took the cup, saying, "This cup is the new covenant in my blood, which is poured out for you. But the hand of him who is going to betray me is with mine on the table. The Son of Man will go as it has been decreed, but woe to that man who betrays him." They began to question among themselves which of them it might be who would do this.

SELECTIONS FROM LUKE

Luke 22:39-48

Jesus went out as usual to the Mount of Olives, and his disciples followed him. On reaching the place, he said to them, "Pray that you will not fall into temptation." He withdrew about a stone's throw beyond them, knelt down and prayed, **"Father, if you are willing, take this cup from me; yet not my will, but yours be done."** An angel from heaven appeared to him and strengthened him. And being in anguish, he prayed more earnestly, and his sweat was like drops of blood falling to the ground.

When he rose from prayer and went back to the disciples, he found them asleep, exhausted from sorrow. "Why are you sleeping?" he asked them. "Get up and pray so that you will not fall into temptation."

While he was still speaking a crowd came up, and the man who was called Judas, one of the Twelve, was leading them. He approached Jesus to kiss him, But Jesus asked him, "Judas, are you betraying the Son of Man with a kiss?"

Luke 22:54

Then seizing him, they led him away and took him into the house of the high priest. Peter followed at a distance.

Luke 22:66-71

At daybreak the council of the elders of the people, both the chief priests and teachers of the law, met together, and Jesus was led before them. "If you are the Christ," they said, "tell us."

Jesus answered, "If I tell you, you will not believe me, and if I asked you, you would not answer. But from now on, the Son of Man will be seated at the right hand of the mighty God."

They all asked, "Are you then the Son of God?" He replied, "You are right in saying I am."

Then they said, "Why do we need any more testimony? We have heard it from his own lips."

Luke 23:1-46

Then the whole assembly rose and led him off to Pilate. And they began to accuse him, saying, "We have found this man subverting our nation. He opposes payment of taxes to Caesar and claims to be Christ, a king."

So Pilate asked Jesus, "Are you the king of the Jews?" "Yes, it is as you say," Jesus replied.

Then Pilate announced to the chief priests and the crowd, "I find no basis for a charge against this man." But they insisted, "He stirs up the people all over Judea by his teaching. He started in Galilee and has come all the way here."

On hearing this, Pilate asked if the man was a Galilean. When he learned that Jesus was under Herod's jurisdiction, he sent him to Herod, who was also in Jerusalem at that time. When Herod saw Jesus, he was greatly pleased, because for a long time he had been wanting to see him. From what he had heard about him, he hoped to see him perform some miracle. He plied him with many questions, but Jesus gave him no answer.

The chief priests and the teachers of the law were standing there, vehemently accusing him. Then Herod and his soldiers ridiculed and mocked him. Dressing him in an elegant robe, they sent him back to Pilate. That day Herod and Pilate became friends—before this they had been enemies.

Pilate called together the chief priests, the rulers and the people, and said to them, "You brought me this man as one who was inciting the people to rebellion. I have examined him in your presence and have found no basis for your charges against him. Neither has Herod, for he sent him back to us; as you can see, he has done nothing to deserve death. Therefore, I will punish him and then release him."

With one voice they cried out, "Away with this man! Release Barabbas to us!" (Barabbas had been thrown into prison for an insurrection in the city, and for murder.) Wanting to release Jesus, Pilate appealed to them again. But they kept shouting, "Crucify him! Crucify him!"

For the third time he spoke to them: "Why? What crime has this man committed? I have found in him no grounds for the death penalty. Therefore I will have him punished and then release him."

But with loud shouts they insistently demanded that he be crucified, and their shouts prevailed. So Pilate decided to grant their demand. He released the man who had been thrown into prison for insurrection and murder, the one they asked for, and surrendered Jesus to their will.

As they led him away, they seized Simon from Cyrene, who was on his way in from the country, and put the cross on him and made him carry it behind Jesus. A large number of people followed him, including women who mourned and wailed for him. Jesus turned and said to them, “Daughters of Jerusalem, do not weep for me; weep for yourselves and for your children. For the time will come when you will say, ‘Blessed are the barren women, the wombs that never bore and the breasts that never nursed!’ Then they will say to the mountains, ‘Fall on us!’ and to the hills, ‘Cover us!’ For if men do these things when the tree is green, what will happen when it is dry?”

Two other men, both criminals, were also led out with him to be executed. When they came to the place called the Skull, there they crucified him, along with the criminals—one on his right, the other on his left. **Jesus said, “Father, forgive them, for they do not know what they are doing.”** And they divided up his clothes by casting lots.

The people stood watching, and the rulers even sneered at him. They said, “He saved others; let him save himself if he is the Christ of God, the Chosen One.”

The soldiers also came up and mocked him. They offered him wine vinegar and said, “If you are the king of the Jews, save yourself.”

There was a written notice above him, which read: THIS IS THE KING OF THE JEWS.

One of the criminals who hung there hurled insults at him: “Aren't you the Christ? Save yourself and us!” But the other criminal rebuked him. “Don't you fear God,” he said, “since you are under the same sentence? We are punished justly, for we are getting what our deeds deserve. But this man has done nothing wrong.”

Then he said, “Jesus, remember me when you come into your kingdom.” **Jesus answered him, “I tell you the truth, today you will be with me in paradise.”**

It was now about the sixth hour, and darkness came over the whole land until the ninth hour, for the sun stopped shining. And the curtain of the temple was torn in two. Jesus called out with a loud voice, **“Father, into your hands I commit my spirit.”** When he had said this, he breathed his last.

THE RESURRECTION

Matthew 28:1-7

After the Sabbath, at dawn on the first day of the week, Mary Magdalene and the other Mary went to look at the tomb.

There was a violent earthquake, for an angel of the Lord came down from heaven and, going to the tomb, rolled back the stone and sat on it. His appearance was like lightning, and his clothes were white as snow. The guards were so afraid of him that they shook and became like dead men.

The angel said to the women, **"Do not be afraid, for I know that you are looking for Jesus, who was crucified. He is not here; he has risen, just as he said.** Come and see the place where he lay. Then go quickly and tell his disciples: 'He has risen from the dead and is going ahead of you into Galilee. There you will see him.' Now I have told you."

Appearances of the Risen Lord

Mark 16:9-16

When Jesus rose early on the first day of the week, he appeared first to Mary Magdalene, out of whom he had driven seven demons. She went and told those who had been with him and who were mourning and weeping. When they heard that Jesus was alive and that she had seen him, they did not believe it.

Afterward Jesus appeared in a different form to two of them while they were walking in the country. These returned and reported it to the rest; but they did not believe them either.

Later Jesus appeared to the Eleven as they were eating; he rebuked them for their lack of faith and their stubborn refusal to believe those who had seen him after he had risen.

He said to them, **"Go into all the world and preach the good news to all creation. Whoever believes and is baptized will be saved, but whoever does not believe will be condemned."**

The Great Commission

Matthew 28:16-20

Then the eleven disciples went to Galilee, to the mountain where Jesus had told them to go. When they saw him, they worshiped him; but some doubted. Then Jesus came to them and said, "All authority in heaven and on earth has been given to me. **Therefore go and make disciples of all nations, baptizing them in the name of the Father and of the Son and of the Holy Spirit, and teaching them to obey everything I have commanded you. And surely I am with you always, to the very end of the age."**

The Ascension

Luke 24:50-53

When he had led them out to the vicinity of Bethany, he lifted up his hands and blessed them. While he was blessing them, he left them and was taken up into heaven. Then they worshiped him and returned to Jerusalem with great joy. And they stayed continually at the temple, praising God.

God Our Refuge

ASKING HIM

Prayers

In that day

you will no longer ask me anything.

I tell you the truth,

my Father will give you

whatever you ask in my name.

— John 16:23

CHRISTIAN PRAYER

In prayer I commune with God. Prayer is my answer to him. God first comes to me in his Holy Word and sacraments where he reveals himself to me as my Creator, my Redeemer, and my Sanctifier. In prayer I answer him. I tell him about all my needs and thank him for all he gives me. In prayer I open my heart to the living God confident that my Father in heaven rejoices to hear my prayer.

Christian prayer is prayer in the name of Jesus. That means that we pray while trusting that Jesus has paid for our sins and that God has accepted us as his dear children.

We know that when we believers pray here on earth, our ascended Lord Jesus prays with us and for us before the Father's throne in heaven. Therefore prayer in his name is effective. Because our Lord hears our prayer and is faithful to answer it according to his wisdom and love, we close our prayers with a firm "Amen," that is "Yes! It shall be so!"

Jesus himself has given us our model prayer: the Lord's Prayer. In it he teaches us to lay all our concerns before our heavenly Father. First, we are to pray regarding spiritual matters pertaining to our souls and to his kingdom, his name, his gracious rule, and his will.

God also invites us to pray regarding our earthly affairs, our daily bread, our trespasses, our temptations, the evil that assaults us. How assuring to hear our Savior promise: *I will do whatever you ask in my name* (John 14:13).

Fixed prayers such as the Lord's Prayer and other treasures from the church's heritage are very helpful for our devotion, but we should also diligently practice spontaneous prayer, prayer spoken from the heart on the basis of a particular Word of God.

It is helpful to set a regular time for our devotions and not be quick to change. Then too, praying out loud may prevent our thoughts from straying. Kneeling and bowing in confession, as well as standing and lifting our heads in praise and adoration are also fine old prayer-customs.

Regardless of our prayer schedule or posture, praying in Jesus' name is God pleasing and helpful. Yes, God himself has invited us to pray and has promised to hear us.

The prayer of a righteous man
is powerful and effective.
— James 5:16

IN ADVENT

See, your king comes to you! — Matthew 21:5

O Lord, send your Holy Spirit to prepare my heart to receive Jesus as my Savior and King. Convict me of my sin and guilt and lead me to genuine repentance. Build me up in my faith with your blessed gospel that I may trust in the merits of my Savior for pardon and salvation. Motivate and empower me to serve you in every way I can. I pray in the name of Jesus, my Redeemer and my King. Amen.

Gracious God, you sent John the Baptist to prepare the hearts of people in times gone by to receive Jesus as their Savior. Use our pastors and missionaries to prepare our hearts for Christ's coming by their proclamation of your law and gospel. Fill our hearts with true peace and joy as we hear the good news that Jesus was born to save us. In Jesus' name. Amen.

Lord Jesus, I praise you for leaving your throne on high to become my brother and my Redeemer. Continue to come to your servant through your Holy Word and sacraments so that I might be prepared to meet you at your final coming at the end of the world. Amen.

In the Christmas Season

The Word became flesh and made his dwelling among us. — John 1:14

Dear Father in heaven, in eternity you planned to send your only Son to rescue fallen mankind. How can I thank you enough for calling me out of the darkness of unbelief into the glorious light of saving faith? What your faithful people in Old Testament times could only dream about, I have seen fulfilled in Jesus. As I worship the Christ Child at this time of his birth, turn my attention from the distractions of this busy world to the glorious truths of the Christmas gospel. With the virgin Mary, let me treasure this gospel in my heart. Like the shepherds, open my mouth to tell others of all that you have done for me. In Jesus' name I pray. Amen.

I thank and praise you, O Christ, for becoming the Son of Man that I might forever be a child of God. Amen.

For Christmas Eve

O Lord, you made this most holy night to shine with the brightness of the true Light. Shine on my darkened heart with his gospel that I may enjoy his peace for time and eternity. In my Savior's name. Amen.

IN THE SEASON OF EPIPHANY

Arise, shine, for your light has come, and the glory of the LORD rises upon you. — Isaiah 60:1

Lord Jesus, just as you revealed yourself as the promised Messiah to the wise men of old, reveal your glory as Lord and Savior to me. As they worshiped you and presented their gifts of gold, frankincense, and myrrh, so lead me to worship and serve you in all that I say and do. Amen.

Dear Savior, use the Bible readings of this season to remind me that you do not want anyone to perish but want everyone to be saved and to come to the knowledge of your truth. To that end, increase my knowledge of your word and strengthen my faith that I might open my mouth and proclaim your praises to my family and community. Cause my light to shine so that others might join me in singing your praises in time and eternity. Amen.

Lord God, centuries ago you led the wise men to their Savior by means of a star. Use your Holy Word to guide me to him once again. Implant in my heart the same kind of love for souls that burned in my Savior's heart as he sacrificed himself to save us. Lead me to devote my time, talents and treasures for the work of his kingdom. Amen.

In Lent

Look, the Lamb of God, who takes away the sin of the world! — John 1:29

Almighty and merciful God, you never despise what you have made and always forgive those who turn to you. During this Lenten season create in me a new and contrite heart that I might always be sorry for my sins and obtain your gracious pardon; through your Son, Jesus Christ my Lord, who lives and reigns with you and the Holy Spirit, one God, now and forever. Amen.

Lord Jesus, with your holy life and innocent death on the cross, you have redeemed the world from sin and eternal death. Have mercy on me and pardon my sin. Amen.

But he was pierced for our transgressions,
he was crushed for our iniquities;
the punishment that brought us
peace was upon him,
and by his wounds we are healed.

We all, like sheep, have gone astray,
each of us has turned to his own way;
and the LORD has laid on him
the iniquity of us all. — Isaiah 53:5-6

For Easter

The Lord has risen! He has risen indeed!
— Luke 24:34

O risen Savior, today I celebrate your resurrection from death and the grave. Have mercy on me and grant that I may rise with you into everlasting life.

After his suffering, he showed himself to these men and gave many convincing proofs that he was alive (Acts 1:3).

O God, you made the dawn of this most holy day shine with the glory of my Lord's resurrection. Through his victory I have been raised from the death of sin. Send me your Holy Spirit that I may worship you with sincerity and truth. As you banished the doubts and fears of your disciples with your words of peace, come and rekindle my faith and trust. In the name of our victorious and risen Savior. Amen.

Almighty God, through your one and only Son you have overcome death and opened to us the gate of everlasting life. I humbly pray that you would fill my heart with the joy of your salvation, that living in Christian love, I might please you in all I say and do. Amen.

At the Ascension of Our Lord

I am returning to my Father and your Father, to my God, and your God. — John 20:17

My Savior, you ascended far above the heavens into the presence of God. As you reminded Thomas, convince me also that you alone are the way, the truth, and the life. Have mercy on me that I might follow you to where you have gone and forever be where you are. Amen.

When he had led them out to the vicinity of Bethany, he lifted up his hands and blessed them. While he was blessing them, he left them and was taken up into heaven. Then they worshiped him and returned to Jerusalem with great joy. And they stayed continually at the temple, praising God (Luke 24:50-53).

Thank you Lord Jesus for ascending on high and for sitting at the right hand of your Father. There you are ruling over all things for the benefit of your people. Jesus, whenever I am surrounded by danger or overwhelmed with trouble, remind me that you remain in control of my life. Enable me to trust in your wisdom and goodness just as a little child trusts his parents. Let me find refuge in you. Amen.

PENTECOST

And I will ask the Father, and he will give you another Counselor to be with you forever—the Spirit of truth. The world cannot accept him, because it neither sees him nor knows him. But you know him, for he lives with you and will be in you. I will not leave you as orphans; I will come to you.
— John 14:16-18

Holy Spirit, God and Lord, come to us this joyful day with your sevenfold gift of grace. Rekindle in our hearts the holy fire of your love that in a true and living faith we may tell abroad the glory of our Savior, Jesus Christ, who lives and reigns with you and the Father, one God, now and forever. Amen.

O Lord, my God, you have revealed yourself in your Holy Word as Father, Son, and Holy Spirit, three persons in one divine being. Father, in eternity you planned to rescue your creation from the ravages of sin and death. Eternal Son of the Father, in mercy you humbled yourself and were born of a virgin, suffered at the hands of your enemies, and poured out your lifeblood on the cross. Send me your Holy Spirit to nurture and sustain my faith through your life-giving Word and Sacraments. Hear my prayer, my Lord and my God. Amen.

On Trinity Sunday

Holy, holy, holy, is the LORD Almighty; the whole earth is full of his glory. — Isaiah 6:3

Eternal and gracious Lord, Father, Son and Holy Spirit, have mercy on me and bless me with your divine presence today and always. Amen.

Holy, holy holy! Lord God Almighty!
Early in the morning our song shall rise to thee;
Holy, holy, holy, merciful and mighty,
God in three persons, blessed Trinity!
(#195 Christian Worship Vs 1)

Almighty God, in love that knows no bounds, you gave your Son so that all who would believe in him might not die but live forevermore. Send me your Holy Spirit so that I might continue steadfast in this faith and attain my heavenly goal. Fix my eyes on Jesus, the author and finisher of my faith. Open my heart to receive him as my only Lord and Savior. Open my lips to praise him for his mercy. Through faith in his merits, I bring my petitions before you. Amen.

O triune God, cleanse our hearts and lips that we might ever worship you, one true immortal God, Father, Son and Holy Spirit. Amen.

For the Church

O Lord God, our heavenly Father, pour out the Holy Spirit on your faithful people. Keep us strong in your grace and truth, protect and comfort us in all temptation, and bestow on us your saving peace, through Jesus Christ, our Lord, who lives and reigns with you and the Holy Spirit, one God, now and forever. Amen.

For Missions

Lord Jesus Christ, you commanded your apostles to preach your gospel to every nation. You did not leave them on their own; rather, you accompanied and blessed their labors as they carried out their glorious task. Send out your truth and your light to the farthest regions of the earth in our day as well. Prepare faithful pastors, teachers and missionaries to preach the gospel in our own land and throughout the world. Guide, protect and prosper their labors so that many others might come to confess you as Savior and serve you with godly living. We ask this in Jesus' name. Amen.

For Absent Loved Ones

O God, our heavenly Father, I commit to your tender care all whom I love, especially those who are far away. O Lord, be with them all. Bless them with good things and keep them from physical harm. Above all, bless and strengthen their souls. Pour out your Holy Spirit on them and guide them into your truth. Remind us to put on your spiritual armor so that we might stand strong and victorious against our enemies. Keep the lamp of our faith burning brightly as we await the final coming of our Lord and Savior. Then, when that blessed day dawns and as we lift up our heads in joy, receive us all into your heavenly kingdom. Grant my prayer, Father, for the sake of your Son, my Lord Jesus Christ. Amen.

For Love

O God, you are love. Enable me to live in love just as Christ has loved me. Penetrate my stony heart with your gospel so that I too might be kind, tenderhearted and forgiving, even as you forgive me for Jesus' sake. Remove all selfishness, bitterness, and arrogance from my heart so that all I say and do might be pleasing in your sight, O Lord, my rock and my Redeemer. Amen.

Show us your unfailing love, O LORD. — Psalm 85:7

A Prayer for Guidance

Father, I know that every good and perfect gift comes from your gracious hand. I pray that you would guide me in my life by the light of your divine Word so that I might think and do those things that are right and good. Give me understanding that I might recognize and avoid the snares and temptations of the evil one. In Jesus. Amen.

When Beginning a Task

My kind and wise God and Lord, you know my weaknesses. Without your strength and guidance all that I plan and do would be for naught. Therefore, assist me with your grace as I approach this task. Direct me by your Word and support me with your power. Give me the necessary insights and diligence that I might succeed and give glory to your holy name. Through Jesus Christ, my Lord. Amen.

In Temptation

Almighty God, wherever I turn, danger is lurking. I am weak and fall victim to Satan's plots all too frequently. Protect me in every danger and support me in every temptation. I am your child. Amen.

For Forgiveness

Merciful Father, grant me grace that I may approach you with a penitent and believing heart. I confess that I have sinned against you and am not worthy to be your child. Yet, I ask you to show mercy and to forgive what I have done wrong for the sake of your Son, Jesus Christ. For his sake, pardon my sin and keep me as your own. And lest I fall victim to this sin in the future, strengthen my faith and empower me with your Holy Spirit so that I might always obey your holy will. Through Jesus Christ, my Lord and Savior. Amen.

For Steadfastness Of Heart

Lord Jesus, friend of sinners, be my friend during this turbulent time. You know all about the storm that has swept over my soul. Ground my heart so firmly in your Word that my faith may never fail. Cause your gospel to shine so brightly in my life that it might cast out the dark shadows of doubt and fear. When Satan approaches me as a lion does its prey, then make me courageous as I fight against him with the sword of your Spirit, your holy Word. Grant peace to my soul for time and eternity. Amen.

Teach me your way, O Lord,
and I will walk in your truth. — Psalm 86:11

In Time of Peril

Remember me, O God, in this hour of utmost need. Prevent my fears from being realized and cause this danger to pass by. Nevertheless, if it is your holy will to place this burden upon me or on those I love, then Lord, grant me strength to bear it and faith to recognize your blessing in it. I pray in the name of my Savior who has promised that he will never leave or forsake me. Amen.

For Peace and Quietness

Lord God, all holy desires, all good counsels, and all just works come from you. Give to us, your servants, that peace which the world cannot give, that our hearts may be set to obey your commandments. Defend us also from the fear of our enemies, that we may live in peace and quietness, through the merits of Jesus Christ, who lives and reigns with you and the Holy Spirit, one God, now and forever. Amen.

May the blessing of the eternal God be upon us:
his light to guide us,
his presence to shelter us,
his peace to unite us. Amen.

For All Who Suffer

O Lord Jesus Christ, you suffered for us and endured even the agony of the cross. Draw near to your suffering servant(s), *[name]* during this time of bodily pain and trouble of mind. During this difficult time, grant him/her safe haven in the shelter of your love. Give them courage to endure and confidence that you will cause even this hardship to work for their spiritual and eternal good. Keep our eyes focused on that glorious kingdom which you established for all who take refuge in your promises. Hear the pleas of your children. Amen.

For Patience

O God, you appointed us to endure suffering and death with our Lord Jesus Christ before we enter into his glory. As we look up to him who suffered for us, do not allow us to grow weary or faint. Instead, invigorate our faith that we might follow in his footsteps and imitate the perseverance of the saints. Provide us with your strength that we may endure in our faith to the end and be saved. Listen to our prayer for Jesus' sake. Amen.

Guide our steps by the light of your Word.
Shield us from harm and keep us from evil.

Thanksgiving for God's Mercy

Gracious God, your mercy is from everlasting to everlasting. Thank you for not dealing with me as I deserve because of my many sins. I praise you for lifting the burden of my guilt from my shoulders and forgiving me those things for which my conscience has made me afraid. I rejoice to hear your words of pardon and peace offered freely to me in Jesus' name. To you, O Lord, I turn. I will always trust in your promise to show mercy. Amen.

For Purity

Compassionate Lord, your strength is made perfect in weakness. Listen to my prayer and answer me. I am neither pure nor perfect. My life has been full of sin and evil. I have no one to blame but myself. But Lord, you have pardoned my sin and cleansed me by your gospel. Through the influence of your Holy Spirit enable me to crucify my sinful flesh and to transform my mind so that it may be in harmony with your own. Grant that I may glorify your holy name in all I say and do. In the name of my perfect and holy Savior. Amen.

The LORD upholds all those who fall
and lifts up all who are bowed down. — Psalm 145:14

For Our Country

Lord of the nations, I praise you for the precious inheritance of this great land. I pray that I and my fellow citizens might ever remain mindful of your blessings and rejoice to do your will. Bless our nation with God-fearing leaders, honorable industry and peace from our enemies. Preserve us from violence of every kind, from discord and confusion, from pride and arrogance, and from every other evil.

Defend our liberties and unite us as one people. Grant wisdom and integrity to all who are entrusted with positions of authority that there may be justice and peace, law and order throughout our great land. Equip and embolden your church on earth to make good use of the blessings you have granted by promoting your gospel in every village and city. In times of prosperity fill our hearts with thankfulness. In times of trouble, do not allow our trust in your providence to fail. Amen.

May God be gracious to us and bless us
and make his face shine upon us;

May your ways be known on earth,
your salvation among all nations. — Psalm 67:1-2

Thanksgiving for One Who Has Died In the Lord

Blessed Lord, you continue to provide for those who have died in faith and finally rest from their labors. Even in my sorrow, I will praise and thank you because [*name*] has finished *his* journey and kept the faith. I know that although *he* is absent from *his* physical body, *he* is at home with you. Comfort me and all who mourn *his* death with the soothing strains of the Easter gospel. I pray trusting that Jesus is my Savior. Amen.

Thanksgiving for the Assurance of Eternal Life

My risen and ascended Savior, I am comforted by your gracious promise: *Do not let your hearts be troubled. Trust in God; trust also in me. In my Father's house are many rooms; if it were not so, I would have told you. I am going there to prepare a place for you. And if I go and prepare a place for you, I will come back and take you to be with me that you also may be where I am* (John 14:1-3). Thank you for this blessed assurance. I will trust and not be afraid. You died and rose again that I might live with you in heaven forevermore. Amen.

Before Holy Communion

This is my body given for you; do this in remembrance of me . . . This cup is the new covenant in my blood, which is poured out for you.
— Luke 22:19-20

Lord, I am not worthy to be a guest at your holy table. But you are the friend of sinners, and you will not cast me out. This bread is your body, which bore my sins upon the tree. This wine is your blood, which purifies me from all guilt. At your invitation, I come rejoicing. Receive me, my Savior. Amen.

After Holy Communion

Thank you, Lord Jesus Christ, for nourishing me in this sacrament with your body and blood. You have given me forgiveness, life, and salvation. Let me always remain in you as a branch remains in the vine. Send me out in the power of your Holy Spirit to live and work to your praise and glory. Amen.

Give thanks to the Lord, for he is good;
his love endures forever! — 1 Chronicles 16:34

God Our Refuge

PRAISING HIM

Hymns

Praise the LORD.

Praise the LORD from the heavens,

praise him in the heights above.

— Psalm 148:1

Sing to the Lord

God's people have delighted to sing spiritual songs in praise of their Lord and Master in every generation. The history of the church is filled with references to the devout practice of hymn singing. Examples of such songs appear in great quantity. Following scriptural suggestions like that of Psalm 149, *Praise the LORD. Sing to the Lord a new song . . .* Christian poets and composers have furnished the church with a splendid heritage of chorales which restate the glorious truth of Scriptures in the musical language of poetry.

The best chorales in this vast heritage are those which most clearly and unequivocally set forth the heart of the gospel, those which deal with the realities of the Christian life and speak unflinchingly of man's dreadful sin and of God's bountiful grace in Christ our Savior.

Many of these hymns have become dear to us. We delight to sing them with fellow believers in worship of our gracious Lord. Yet the use of our hymns has not been exploited fully if we only sing them in formal public worship. The treasury of our chorales ought to also have a place in our private devotion. We stand in daily need of the precious comfort and en- couragement which they offer during the changing circumstances of life on earth. Besides, there is much to be learned from our hymns regarding the only way of salvation.

The following pages contain a selection of chorale stanzas chosen for their quality and their applicability to personal worship such as you are contemplating. The hymns on the next twelve pages are arranged according to the seasons of the church year. Those that follow are helpful in a variety of situations and are not arranged in any particular order.

O Lord, How Shall I Meet You,
How welcome you aright?
Your people long to greet you,
My Hope, my heart's Delight.
O Jesus, let your Word be
A lamp to light my way,
To show me how to please you,
To guide me ev'ry day.

Love caused your incarnation;
Love brought you down to me.
Your thirst for my salvation
Procured my liberty.
Oh, love beyond all telling
That led you to embrace
In love, all love excelling,
Our lost and fallen race!

Rejoice, then, you sad-hearted,
Who sit in deepest gloom,
Who mourn o'er joys departed
And tremble at your doom.
Despair not; he is near you,
He's standing at the door
Who best can help and cheer you
And bids you weep no more.

He comes to judge the nations,
A terror to his foes,
A light of consolations,
And blessed hope to those
Who love the Lord's appearing.
O glorious Sun, now come,
Send forth your beams most cheering,
And guide us safely home.
(#18, 19 Christian Worship Vs 1-3, 5)

From Heaven Above to Earth I Come
To bear good news to ev'ry home;
Glad tidings of great joy I bring,
Whereof I now will say and sing:

To you this night is born a child
Of Mary, chosen virgin mild;
This little child of lowly birth
Shall be the joy of all the earth.

This is the Christ, our God most high,
Who hears your sad and bitter cry;
He will himself your Savior be
From all your sins to set you free.

How glad we'll be to find it so!
Then with the shepherds let us go
To see what God for us has done
In sending us his own dear Son.

Welcome to earth, O noble Guest,
Through whom the sinful world is blest!
You came to share my misery,
That you might share your joy with me.

Ah, dearest Jesus, holy Child,
Prepare a bed, soft, undefiled
Within my heart, made clean and new,
A quiet chamber kept for you.

Glory to God in highest heaven,
Who unto us his Son has given!
While angels sing with pious mirth
A glad new year to all the earth.
(#38 Christian Worship Vs 1-3, 6, 8, 13, 15)

Savior of the Nations, Come
Virgin's Son, make here your home.
Marvel now, O heav'n and earth,
That the Lord chose such a birth.

Not by human flesh and blood,
By the Spirit of our God
Was the Word of God made flesh,
Woman's offspring, pure and fresh.

From the Father's throne he came
And ascended to the same,
Captive leading death and hell—
High the song of triumph swell!
(#2 Christian Worship Vs 1-2, 4)

Let All Together Praise Our God
Before his highest throne;
Today he opens heav'n again
And gives us his own Son,
And gives us his own Son.

He leaves his heav'nly Father throne,
Is born an infant small,
And in a manger, poor and lone,
Lies in a humble stall,
Lies in a humble stall.

For us he opens wide the door
Of paradise today.
The angel guards the gate no more;
To God our thanks we pay,
To God our thanks we pay.
(#41 Christian Worship Vs. 1-2, 6)

O Sacred Head, Now Wounded
With grief and shame weighed down,
Now scornfully surrounded,
With thorns your only crown,
O sacred head, no glory
Now from your face does shine;
Yet though despised and gory,
I joy to call you mine.

My burden in your passion,
Lord, you have borne for me,
For it was my transgression,
My shame, on Calvary.
I cast me down before you;
Wrath is my rightful lot.
Have mercy, I implore you;
Redeemer, spurn me not!

Lord, be my consolation,
My shield when I must die;
Remind me of your passion
When my last hour draws nigh.
My eyes will then behold you,
Upon your cross will dwell;
My heart will then enfold you—
Who dies in faith dies well!
(#105 Christian Worship Vs 1, 4, 7)

When O'er my Sins I Sorrow
Lord, I will look to you
And hence my comfort borrow
That you were slain for me.
Your precious blood was offered
For me, oh, most unworthy,
To take away my guilt.

Oh, what a marv'lous off'ring!
Behold, the Master spares
His servants, and their suff'ring
And grief for them he bears.
Our God comes down from heaven;
For me, his guilty creature,
He deigns as man to die.

My manifold transgression
Henceforth can harm me none
Since Jesus' bloody passion
For me God's grace has won.
His blood my debt has canceled;
Of hell and all its torments
I am no more afraid.

Therefore I will forever
Give thanks continually,
O Jesus, loving Savior,
For what you did for me.
I'll spend my breath in praises

For your sad cry, your suff'rings,
Your wounds, your guiltless death.
(#109 Christian Worship Vs 1-4)

Awake, My Heart, with Gladness!
See what today is done;
Now, after gloom and sadness,
Comes forth the glorious sun.
My Savior there was laid
Where our bed must be made
When to the realms of light
Our spirit wings its flight.

The foe in triumph shouted
When Christ lay in the tomb.
But lo, he now is routed;
His boast is turned to gloom.
For Christ again is free;
In glorious victory
He who is strong to save
Has triumphed o'er the grave.

Now I will cling forever
To Christ, my Savior true;
My Lord will leave me never,
Whate'er he passes through.
He rends death's iron chain;
He breaks through sin and pain.

He shatters hell's dark thrall;
I follow him through all.

He brings me to the portal
That leads to bliss untold,
Whereon this rhyme immortal
Is found in script of gold:
"Who there my cross has shared
Finds here a crown prepared;
Who there with me has died
Shall here be glorified."
(#156 Christian Worship Vs 1-2, 4-5)

Jesus Christ, My Sure Defense
And my Savior, now is living!
Knowing this, my confidence
Rests upon the hope he's giving,
Though the night of death be fraught
Still with many an anxious thought.

Jesus, my Redeemer, lives;
I, too, unto life shall waken.
Endless joy my Savior gives;
Shall my courage, then, be shaken?
Shall I fear, or could the head
Rise and leave his members dead?

No, too closely am I bound
Unto him by hope forever;
Faith's strong hand the rock has found,
Grasped it, and will leave it never.
Even death now cannot part
From its Lord the trusting heart.
(#167 Christian Worship Vs 1-3)

On Christ's Ascension
The hope of my ascension.
This hope alone has always stilled
All doubt and apprehension;
For where the head is, there as well I know his members are to dwell
When Christ shall come and call them.

Since Christ returned to claim his throne,
Great gifts for me obtaining,
My heart shall rest in him alone,
No other rest remaining,
For where my treasure went before, There all my thoughts shall ever soar
To still their deepest yearning.

Oh, grant, dear Lord, this grace to me,
Recalling your ascension,
That I may serve you faithfully,
Adorning your redemption;
And then, when all my days will cease,

Let me depart in joy and peace
In answer to my pleading.
(#173 Christian Worship Vs 1-3)

Hail the Day that Sees Him Rise
To his throne above the skies!
Christ, the Lamb for sinners giv'n,
Re-ascends his native heav'n.

There the glorious triumph waits:
Lift your heads, eternal gates.
He has conquered death and sin;
Take the King of glory in!

See, the heav'n its Lord receives,
Yet he loves the earth he leaves;
Though returning to his throne,
Still he calls mankind his own.

See he lifts his hands above;
See, he shows the prints of love,
Hark! His gracious lips bestow
Blessings on his Church below.

Still for us he intercedes;
His prevailing death he pleads.
He, the first of all our race,
Near himself prepares a place.

There we shall with you remain
Partners in your endless reign,
There your face unclouded view,
Find our heav'n of heav'ns in you.
(#175 Christian Worship Vs 1-6)

Come, Holy Ghost, God and Lord
May all your graces be outpoured
On each believer's mind and heart;
Your fervent love to them impart.
Lord, by the brightness of your light
In holy faith your church unite
From ev'ry land and ev'ry tongue;
This to your praise, O Lord our God, be sung:
Alleluia! Alleluia!

Come, holy Fire, Comfort true;
Grant us the will your work to do
And in your service to abide;
Let trials turn us not aside.
Lord, by your pow'r prepare each heart,
And to our weakness strength impart
That bravely here we may contend,
Through life and death to you, our Lord, ascend.
Alleluia! Alleluia!
(#176 Christian Worship Vs 1-3)

We All Believe in One True God,
Who created earth and heaven,
The Father, who to us in love
Has the right of children given.
He in soul and body feed us;
All we need his hand provides us.
He through snares and perils leads us,
Watching that no harm betides us.
He cares for us by day and night;
All things are governed by his might.

We all believe in Jesus Christ,
His own Son, our Lord, possessing
An equal God-head, throne and might,
Source of ev'ry grace and blessing,
Born of Mary, virgin mother,
By the power of the Spirit,
Made true man, our elder brother,
That the lost might life inherit,
Was crucified by sinful men
And raised by God to life again.

We all confess the Holy Ghost,
Who, sweet hope and comfort giving,
Now with the Father and the Son
In eternal light is living,
Who the Church his own creation,
Keeps in unity of spirit;
Here forgiveness and salvation

Daily come through Jesus' merit.
All flesh shall rise, and we shall be
In bliss with God eternally.
(#271 Christian Worship Vs 1-3)

A Mighty Fortress Is Our God
A trusty shield and weapon;
He helps us free from every need
That has us now o'er taken.
The old evil foe
Now means deadly woe;
Deep guile and great might;
Are his dread arms in fight;
On earth is not his equal.

With might of ours can naught be done,
Soon were our loss effected;
But for us fights the valiant one,
Whom God himself elected.
You ask, "Who is this?"
Jesus Christ it is,
The almighty Lord.
And there's no other God:
He holds the field forever.

The Word they still shall let remain,
Nor any thanks have for it;
He's by our side upon the plain
With his good gifts and Spirit.

And do what they will—
Hate, steal, hurt, or kill—
Though all may be gone,
Our victory is won;
The kingdom's ours forever!
(#200, 201 Christian Worship Vs 1-2, 4)

Jesus, Priceless Treasure
Fount of purest pleasure,
Truest friend to me.
Ah, how long in anguish
Shall my spirit languish,
Yearning, Lord, for thee?
Thou art mine, O Lamb divine!
I will suffer naught to hide thee,
Naught I ask beside thee.

In thine arms I rest me;
Foes who would molest me
Cannot reach me here.
Though the earth be shaking,
Ev'ry heart be quaking,
Jesus calms my fear.
Lightnings flash And thunders crash;
Yet tho' sin and hell assail me,
Jesus will not fail me.

Hence, all fear and sadness!
For the Lord of gladness,

Jesus, enters in.
Those who love the Father,
Though the storms may gather,
Still have peace within.
Yea, whate'er I here must bear,
Thou art still my purest pleasure,
Jesus, priceless treasure!
(#349 Christian Worship Vs. 1, 2, 5)

Lord, to You I Make Confession
I have sinned and gone astray
I have multiplied transgression,
Chosen for myself my way.
Led by you to see my errors,
Lord, I tremble at your terrors.

Yet, though conscience' voice appall me,
Father, I will seek your face.
Though your child I dare not call me,
Yet receive me to your grace.
Do not for my sins forsake me;
Do not let your wrath o'ertake me.

For your Son has suffered for me,
Giv'n himself to rescue me,
Died to save me and restore me,
Reconciled and set me free,
Jesus' cross alone can vanquish
These dark fears and sooth this anguish.

Lord, on you I cast my burden—
Sink it in the depths below!
Let me know your gracious pardon;
Wash me, make me white as snow.
Let your Spirit leave me never;
Make me only yours forever.
(#302 Christian Worship Vs 1-4)

I Am Trusting You, Lord Jesus
Trusting only you,
Trusting you for full salvation,
Free and true.

I am trusting you for pardon;
At your feet I bow,
For your grace and tender mercy
Trusting now.

I am trusting you to guide me;
You alone shall lead,
Ev'ry day and hour supplying
All my need.
(#446 Christian Worship Vs 1, 2, 4)

Who Trusts in God, a Strong Abode
In heav'n and earth possesses;
Who looks in love To Christ above—
No fear his heart oppresses.
In you alone, Dear Lord, we own
Sweet hope and consolations,
Our shield from foes, Our balm for woes,
Our great and sure salvation.

In all the strife Of mortal life
Our feet will stand securely.
Temptation's hour Will lose its pow'r,
For you will guard us surely.
O God, renew With heav'nly dew
Our body, soul, and spirit
Until we stand At your right hand
Through Jesus' saving merit.
(#447 Christian Worship Vs 1, 3)

Lord, Take My Hand and Lead Me
Upon life's way;
Direct, protect, and feed me
From day to day.
Without your grace and favor I go astray;
So take my hand, O Savior,
And lead the way.

Lord, when the tempest rages,
I need not fear;
For you, the Rock of Ages,
Are always near.
Close by your side abiding, I fear no foe,
For when your hand is guiding,
In peace I go.

Lord, when the shadows lengthen
And night has come,
I know that you will strengthen
My steps toward home,
And nothing can impede me, O blessed Friend!
So take my hand and lead me
Unto the end.
(#439 Christian Worship Vs 1-3)

Lord Keep Us Steadfast in Your Word;
Curb those who by deceit or sword
Would seek to over throw your Son
And to destroy what he has done.

Lord Jesus Christ, your pow'r make known,
For you are Lord of lords alone;
Defend your Christendom that we
May sing your praise eternally.

O Comforter of priceless worth,
Send peace and unity on earth.
Support us in our final strife,
And lead us out of death to life.
(#203 Christian Worship Vs 1-3)

Dear Christians, One and All, Rejoice
With exultation springing,
And with united heart and voice
And holy rapture singing,
Proclaim the wonders God has done,
How his right arm the vict'ry won.
How dearly it has cost him!

Fast bound in Satan's chains I lay;
Death brooded darkly o'er me.
Sin was my torment night and day;
In sin my mother bore me.
Yet deep and deeper still I fell;
Life had became a living hell,
So firmly sin possessed me.

My own good works availed me naught,
No merit they attaining;
My will against God's judgment fought,
No hope for me remaining.
My fears increased till sheer despair
Left naught but death to be my share
And hell to be my sentence.

But God beheld my wretched state
Before the world's foundation,
And, mindful of his mercies great,
He planned my soul's salvation.
A Father's heart he turned to me,
Sought my redemption fervently;
He gave his dearest treasure.
(#377 Christian Worship Vs 1-4)

With the Lord Begin Your Task
Jesus will direct it.
For his aid and counsel ask;
Jesus will perfect it.
Ev'ry morn with Jesus rise,
And, when day is ended,
In his name then close your eyes;
Be to him commended.

Let each day begin with prayer,
Praise and adoration.
On the Lord cast ev'ry care;
He is your salvation.
Morning, evening, and at night
Jesus will be near you,
Save you from the tempter's might,
With his presence cheer you.

With your Savior at your side
Foes need not alarm you;
In his promises confide
And no ill can harm you.
All your trust and hope repose
In the mighty Master,
Who in wisdom truly knows
How to stem disaster.

If your task is thus begun
With the Savior's blessing,
Safely then your course will run,
Naught your soul distressing.
Good will follow ev'rywhere
While you here must wander;
You at last the joy will share
In the mansions yonder.
(#478 Christian Worship Vs 1-4)

In God, My Faithful God
I trust when dark my road;
Though many woes o'ertake me,
Yet he will not forsake me.
Though heavy griefs are pressing,
He'll turn them into blessing.

My sins assail me sore,
But I despair no more.
I build on Christ, who loves me;
From this rock nothing moves me.
To him I all surrender,
To him, my soul's defender.

If death my portion be,
Then death is gain for me
And Christ my life forever,
From whom death cannot sever.
Come when it may, he'll shield me;
To him I gladly yield me.

"So be it, then," I say
With all my heart each day.
We, too, dear Lord, adore you;
We sing for joy before you.
Guide us while here we wander
Until we praise you yonder.
(#438 Christian Worship Vs 1-4)

Now Rest Beneath Night's Shadow
The woodland, field, and meadow;
The world in slumber lies.
But you, my heart, awaken,
With prayer and song be taken;
Let praise to your Creator rise.

Lord Jesus, since you love me,
Oh, spread your wings above me
And shield me from alarm.
Though Satan would assail me,
Your mercy will not fail me;
I rest in your protecting arm.

My loved ones, rest securely,
For God this night will surely
From peril guard your heads.
Sweet slumbers may he send you
And bid his hosts attend you
And through the night watch o'er your beds.
(#587 Christian Worship Vs 1, 3, 4)

Your Forever, God of Love
Hear us from your throne above:
Yours forever may we be
Here and in eternity!

Yours forever, oh, how blest
They who find in you their rest!
Savior, Guardian, heav'nly Friend,
Oh, defend us to the end.

Yours forever, Lord of life!
Shield us through our earthly strife.
You, the life, the truth, the way,
Guide us to the realms of day.

Yours forever! Shepherd, keep
All your weak and trembling sheep
Safely in your tender care;
Let us all your goodness share.

Yours forever! You our guide,
All our needs by you supplied,
All our sins by you forgiv'n,
Lead us, Lord, from earth to heav'n.
(#426 Christian Worship Vs 1-5)

God Our Refuge

ABIDING IN HIM

Spiritual Treasures

See that what you have heard

from the beginning remains in you.

If it does, you also will remain in the Son

and in the Father.

— John 2:24

ABIDING IN HIM

See that what you have heard from the beginning remains in you. If it does, you also will remain in the Son and in the Father.

—1 John 2:24

We have sought and found our refuge in his Word and sacraments; we have offered our hymns and prayers to him for the wondrous salvation he has wrought. Now it becomes our steadfast purpose to abide in him always, ever grounding our faith on the rock that cannot be moved.

We abide in him as we continue in his Word. Only if we remain in the truth revealed in Scripture shall we abide in him who is our fortress and strong deliverer.

In our well-thumbed catechism and in the familiar liturgy of our Church we find masterful expressions of the faith and hope and joy that live in our hearts as we continue in his Word. As they repeat the central truths of Scripture for us in words familiar to us since our youth, they aid in keeping us faithful to the author and finisher of our faith. Use these well-known gems from the catechism and the liturgy. Let them direct you to his Word and to him who is your refuge.

FROM LUTHER'S SMALL CATECHISM

THE FIRST ARTICLE

My Heavenly Father Provides for Me

I believe in God the Father Almighty, Maker of heaven and earth.

What does this mean?

I believe that God made me and every creature and that he gave me my body and soul, eyes, ears and all my members, my mind and all my abilities.

And I believe that God still preserves me by richly and daily providing clothing and shoes, food and drink, house and home, wife and children, land, cattle and all I own, and all that I need to keep my body and life, and by defending me against all danger and guarding and protecting me from all evil.

All this God does only because he is my good and merciful Father in heaven, and not because I have earned or deserved it.

For all this I ought to thank and praise, to serve and obey him. This is most certainly true.

THE SECOND ARTICLE

My Savior Has Made Me His Own by Dying for Me

I believe in Jesus Christ, his only Son, our Lord: who was conceived by the Holy Ghost; born of the virgin Mary; suffered under Pontius Pilate; was crucified, dead and buried; he descended into hell; the third day he rose again from the dead; he ascended into heaven, and is sitting at the right hand of God the Father Almighty; from there he shall come to judge the living and the dead.

What does this mean?

I believe that Jesus Christ, true God, begotten of the Father from eternity, and also true man, born of the Virgin Mary, is my Lord.

He has redeemed me, a lost and condemned creature, purchased and won me from all sins, from death and from the power of the devil, not with gold or silver, but with his holy, precious blood and with his innocent suffering and death.

All this he did that I should be his own, and live under him in his kingdom, and serve him in ever- lasting righteousness, innocence and blessedness, just as he has risen from death and lives and rules eternally.

This is most certainly true.

THE THIRD ARTICLE

The Holy Spirit Keeps Me in the Saving Faith Which He Has Worked in Me

I believe in the Holy Ghost; the holy Christian church, the communion of saints; the forgiveness of sins; the resurrection of the body; and the life everlasting. Amen.

What does this mean?

I believe that I cannot by my own thinking or choosing believe in Jesus Christ, my Lord, or come to him.

But the Holy Ghost has called me by the gospel, enlightened me with his gifts, sanctified and kept me in the true faith. In the same way he calls, gathers, enlightens, and sanctifies the whole Christian church on earth, and keeps it with Jesus Christ in the one true faith.

In this Christian church he daily and fully forgives all sins to me and all believers.

On the Last Day he will raise me and all the dead; and he will give eternal life to me and all believers in Christ.

This is most certainly true.

The Introduction to the Lord's Prayer

God has Given Me Confidence to Pray by Making Me His Child

Our Father who art in heaven.

What does this mean?

With these words God tenderly invites us to believe that he is our true Father and that we are his true children, so that we may pray to him as boldly and confidently as dear children ask their dear father.

The Lord's Prayer

The Prayer My Savior Has Taught Me to Pray

Our Father in heaven, hallowed be your name your kingdom come your will be done on earth as it is in heaven. Give us today our daily bread. Forgive us our sins as we forgive those who sin against us. Lead us not into temptation but deliver us from evil. For the kingdom, the power and the glory are yours now and forever. Amen.

The Sacrament Of Holy Baptism

God Himself Has Ordained My Baptism

What is Baptism?

Baptism is not just plain water, but it is water used by God's command and connected with God's Word.

What is that Word of God?

Christ our Lord says in the last chapter of Matthew, "Go and make disciples of all nations, baptizing them in the name of the Father and of the Son and of the Holy Spirit!"

My Baptism Gives Me Salvation

What does Baptism do for us?

Baptism works forgiveness of sin, delivers from death and the devil and gives eternal salvation to all who believe this, as the words and promises of God declare.

What is God's promise?

Christ our Lord says in the last chapter of Mark, "Whoever believes and is baptized will be saved, but whoever does not believe will be condemned."

My Baptism Is a Precious Means of Grace

How can water do such great things?

It is certainly not the water that does such things, but God's Word which is in and with the water, and faith which trusts this Word used with the water.

For without God's Word the water is just plain water and not baptism. But with his Word it is baptism. God's Word makes it a washing through which God graciously forgives our sin and grants us rebirth and a new life through the Holy Spirit.

Where is this written?

St. Paul says in Titus, chapter 3, "He saved us through the washing of rebirth and renewal by the Holy Spirit, whom he poured out on us generously through Jesus Christ our Savior, so that, having been justified by his grace, we might become heirs having the hope of eternal life. This is a trustworthy saying."

Here we bring a child of nature;
Home we take a newborn creature,
Now God's precious son or daughter,
Born again by Word and water.
(#300 Christian Worship Vs 4)

My Baptism Is My Stay in My Daily Life of Repentance

What does baptizing with water mean?

It means that our Old Adam with his evil deeds and desires should be drowned by daily contrition and repentance, and die, and that day by day a new man should arise, as from the dead, to live in the presence of God in righteousness and purity now and forever.

Where is this written?

St. Paul says in Romans, chapter 6, "We were therefore buried with him through baptism into death in order that, just as Christ was raised from the dead through the glory of the Father, we too may live a new life."

Baptized into your name most holy,
O Father, Son, and Holy Ghost,
I claim a place, though weak and lowly,
Among your saints, your chosen host,
Buried with Christ and dead to sin.
Your Spirit now shall live within. Amen.
(#294 Christian Worship Vs 1)

THE SACRAMENT OF HOLY COMMUNION

The Sure Foundation of My Faith in the Lord's Supper

What is the sacrament of Holy Communion?

It is the true body and blood of our Lord Jesus Christ together with the bread and wine, instituted by Christ for us Christians to eat and to drink.

Where is this written?

The holy Evangelists Matthew, Mark, Luke and the Apostle Paul tell us: The Lord Jesus, on the night he was betrayed, took bread; and when he had given thanks, he broke it, gave it to his disciples and said, "Take and eat. This is my body, which is given for you; do this in remembrance of me."

In the same way, after supper he took the cup, gave thanks, gave it to them and said, "Drink from it, all of you. This cup is the new covenant in my blood, which is poured out for you for the forgiveness of sins. Do this, whenever you drink it, in remembrance of me."

Draw near and take the body of the Lord,
And drink the holy blood for you outpoured.

Offered was he for greatest and for least,
Himself the victim and himself the priest.
(#309 Christian Worship Vs 1)

My Great Blessings in the Lord's Supper

What blessing do we receive through this eating and drinking?

That is shown us by these words, "Given and poured out for you for the forgiveness of sins."

Through these words we receive forgiveness of sins, life and salvation in this sacrament.

For where there is forgiveness of sins, there is also life and salvation.

This Holy Sacrament Is a Precious Means of Grace

How can eating and drinking do such great things?

It is certainly not the eating and drinking that does such things, but the words, "Given and poured out for you for the forgiveness of sins."

These words are the main thing in this sacrament, along with the eating and drinking.

And whoever believes these words has what they plainly say, the forgiveness of sins.

The Blessed Benefits of the Lord's Supper Are Mine by Faith

Who, then, is properly prepared to receive this sacrament?

Fasting and other outward preparations may serve a good purpose, but he is properly prepared who believes these words, "Given and poured out for you for the forgiveness of sins."

But whoever does not believe these words or doubts them is not prepared, because the words "for you" require nothing but hearts that believe.

From The Liturgy

THE CONFESSION OF SINS

I Have Sinned Against the Lord

Holy and merciful Father, I confess that I am by nature sinful, and that I have disobeyed you in my thoughts, words, and actions. I have done what is evil and failed to do what is good. For this I deserve your punishment both now and in eternity. But I am truly sorry for my sins, and trusting in my Savior Jesus Christ, I pray: Lord, have mercy on me, a sinner.

THE ABSOLUTION

The Lord Has Forgiven My Sin

God our heavenly Father, has been merciful to us and has given his only Son to be the atoning sacrifice for our sins. Therefore, as a called servant of Christ and by his authority, I forgive you all your sins in the name of the Father and of the Son and of the Holy Spirit. Amen.

THE GLORIA IN EXCELSIS

Glory be to God on high,
and on earth peace,
good will toward men.

We praise you, We bless you,
We worship you, We glorify you,
We give thanks to you,
For your great glory.

O Lord God, heav'nly King,
God the Father almighty.
O Lord, the only begotten Son, Jesus Christ;
O Lord God, Lamb of God, Son of the Father,
You take away the sin of the world;
Have mercy on us.
You take away the sin of the world;
Receive our prayer.
You sit at the right hand of God the Father;
Have mercy on us.

For you only are holy;
You only are the Lord.
You only, O Christ, with the Holy Spirit,
Are most high in the glory of God the Father. Amen

THE NICENE CREED

My Faith In the Triune God

We believe in one God, the Father, the Almighty, maker of heaven and earth, of all that is seen and unseen.

We believe in one Lord, Jesus Christ, the only Son of God, eternally begotten of the Father, God from God, Light from Light, true God from true God, begotten, not made, of one being with the Father. Through him all things were made. For us and for our salvation, he came down from heaven, was incarnate of the Holy Spirit and the virgin Mary, and became fully human.

For our sake he was crucified under Pontius Pilate. He suffered death and was buried. On the third day he rose again in accordance with the Scriptures. He ascended into heaven and is seated at the right hand of the Father. He will come again in glory to judge the living and the dead, and his kingdom will have no end.

We believe in the Holy Spirit, the Lord, the giver of life, who proceeds from the Father and the Son, who in unity with the Father and the Son is worshipped and glorified, who has spoken through the prophets.

We believe in one holy Christian and apostolic Church. We acknowledge one baptism for the forgiveness of sins. We look for the resurrection of the dead and the life of the world to come. Amen.

THE OFFERTORY

Create in me a clean heart, O God, and renew a right spirit within me. Cast me not away from your presence, and take not your Holy Spirit from me. Restore unto me the joy of your salvation, and uphold me with your free Spirit. Amen.

THE SANCTUS

My Joyous Welcome to the Conqueror of My Sin

Holy, holy, holy Lord God of heavenly hosts: heav'n and earth are full of your glory. Hosanna, hosanna, hosanna in the highest. Blessed is he, blessed is he, blessed is he who comes in the name of the Lord. Hosanna, hosanna, hosanna in the highest.

THE AGNUS DEI

(The Lamb of God)

My Plea for Pardon and Peace In the Lamb of God

O Christ, Lamb of God, you take away the sin of the world; have mercy on us.

O Christ, Lamb of God, you take away the sin of the world; have mercy on us.

O Christ, Lamb of God, you take away the sin of the world; grant us your peace. Amen.

THE NUNC DIMITTIS

My Soul Is at Peace After God Has Blessed Me Through His Word and Sacraments

Lord, now you let your servant depart in peace according to your word. For my eyes have seen your salvation, which you have prepared before the face of all people, a light to lighten the Gentiles and the glory of your people Israel.

THE BENEDICTION

The Lord bless you and keep you.
The Lord make his face shine on you
and be gracious to you.
The Lord look on you with favor
and give you peace. Amen.